GHOST STORIES *of* LOUISIANA

Dan Asfar

Lone Pine Publishing International

The Publisher: Lone Pine Publishing International
Distributed by Lone Pine Publishing
1808 B Street NW, Suite 140
Auburn, WA 98001
USA

Websites: www.lonepinepublishing.com
www.ghostbooks.net

National Library of Canada Cataloguing in Publication Data

Asfar, Dan, 1973-
 Ghost stories of Louisiana / Dan Asfar.

  ISBN-13: 978-1-894877-19-0
  ISBN-10: 1-894877-19-5

  1. Ghosts-Louisiana. 2. Tales—Louisiana. I. Title.

GR110.L5A83 2007   398.2'09763'05   C2005-904485-3

Photo Credits: Every effort has been made to accurately credit photographers. Any errors or omissions should be directed to the publisher for changes in future editions. The photographs and illustrations in this book are reproduced with the kind permission of the following sources: Dan Asfar (pp. 4-5, p. 27, 44, 63, 72, 89, 115, 119, 171, 178, 184, 187, 193, 202); Istock (p. 65: Annene Kaye; p. 95: Joseph Jean Dube; p. 102: Erik Gauger; p. 124: Lise Gagne); Library of Congress (p. 10, 49: USZC4-4841; p. 36: B8172-1406; p. 168: HABS, LA,36-NEWOR,13-4; p. 175: B813-1685 A-1; p. 199: USZ62-15627); Myrtles Plantation (p. 14).

The stories, folklore and legends in this book are based on the author's collection of sources including individuals whose experiences have led them to believe they have encountered phenomena of some kind or another. They are meant to entertain, and neither the publisher nor the author claims these stories represent fact.

PC: P5

To Curt and Elliot,
the pillars of production

CONTENTS

Acknowledgments 6
Introduction 7

Chapter One: Plantation Phantoms and Haunted Houses

The Ghosts of the Myrtles Plantation 11
The Haunted House 25
The Singing in the Attic 35
The Andrew Jackson Hotel 43
The Ghosts of Oak Alley Plantation 46
Lloyd Hall Plantation 54

Chapter Two: Dark Legends of Louisiana

Voodoo in New Orleans 64
The Spirit of Marie Laveau 67
The Ghost of the Raccourci Cut-off 80
The Sultan's Palace 84
Le Mythe du Loup-Garou 94
Run Off the Road 99
The Bigfoot of Kisatchie 101

Chapter Three: Local Tales and Ghostly Memoirs

"She Was Standing by the River" 116
A Grandmother's Return 127
Blood and Tears on Potter Road 134
The Wooden Hunter 136
Haunting in Baton Rouge 144
A Spirit in the Woods? 150
Murder in the Red Barn 157
An Uptown Haunting 159

Chapter Four: Spirits of the Past

The Bells of Chartres Street 169
Little Napoleon 173
The Curve in the Tracks 181
Père Dagobert and the Phantom Funeral Procession 182
The Taylortown Tower 189
The Ghost of Père Antoine and the St. Louis Cathedral 191
The Pirate Jean Lafitte 195

Acknowledgments

First and foremost, thanks go to those who stepped forward and shared their experiences with me. Though most of you preferred to remain anonymous, your accounts were greatly appreciated and added much to the stories in this volume. In addition, it would be remiss of me to neglect acknowledging the paranormal storytellers who have covered the subject of ghosts in Louisiana. Barbara Sillery's *The Haunting of Louisiana*, Robert Tallant's *Voodoo in New Orleans*, Christy L. Viviano's *Haunted Louisiana*, Jill Pascoe's *Louisiana's Haunted Plantations*, Victor C. Klein's *New Orleans Ghosts*, Katherine Smith's *Journey into Darkness...Ghosts and Vampires of New Orleans* and, of course, Troy Taylor's *Haunted New Orleans: Ghosts & Hauntings of the Crescent City* have all inspired and informed more than one of the stories in this book.

Thanks go, as well, to the people at Ghost House. Kudos to Wendy Pirk and Rachelle Delaney, two fine editors, and Carol Woo, for supplementing the text with the photos. Thanks.

Introduction

There's a bit of a story to this book. Slated for release in the fall of 2005, the manuscript was completed and sent to the printer in August of that year. Then, on the morning of August 29, everything changed.

Just after 6 AM, Hurricane Katrina swept in. At category 3, with 125-mile-per-hour winds churning up storm tides over 14 feet, she wreaked destruction all along the southeast coast of Louisiana. Bay St. Louis, Poplarville and Waveland were all hit, but it was her path through New Orleans that got the world's attention. The ensuing broken levees, flooded streets and chaos created an unfolding calamity was ugly, tragic and revealing.

The immediate decision to postpone the release of this book required no discussion. With the entire country struggling to come to terms with what had happened, to release a book of Louisiana ghost stories would have been profoundly inappropriate and disrespectful. The printer was called. *Ghost Stories of Louisiana* was postponed.

Until now. New Orleans has begun to heal. Although much of the eastern part of the city is still in ruins, the center has been up and running for some time. The bars and restaurants are open. There is music in the French Quarter. And the ghost stories of the famously haunted city are being told once more.

The stories are being told the same way as they were before Katrina, by local paranormal enthusiasts and storytellers leading tour groups through the streets after sunset, introducing visitors to the city's ghosts by the dim glow of streetlights. These caretakers of New Orleans' ghost stories are ready to put Katrina behind them.

"What happened doesn't come up too much in the tours," says Mike Indesg of New Orleans Ghost Tours. "There's one story out there about a national guardsman who saw a spirit when he went in to one of the houses, but we don't talk about the storm. Maybe in 100 years, there'll be stories going around. That's not what we want now. More than anything, we want people to start coming back here. People think that the city is wasted and that it's dangerous. It isn't true. We're back up and ready for business."

Sydney Smith, owner of Haunted History Tours, is also ready to move forward, but he's frustrated that visitors have been slow to return to this formerly popular tourist destination. "I blame the news media," he says. "All we get are stories of how there's no law here and we've got gangs running free. It isn't true." A New Orleans resident who stayed in his home through the hurricane, Smith will not incorporate any stories of Katrina in his tour. "People on the tour don't really ask about it, and I don't go there."

Ghosts have long been part of New Orleans' attractions, along with the vibrant music scene, the world-famous food and the dizzying hedonism of Bourbon Street. Countless spirits of the legendary dead are said to drift through the city's gorgeously decaying French Quarter's streets and haunt its buildings. No one, however—not even me—is ready to talk about the ghosts of Katrina. Although tragedy and untimely death form a common theme in ghost stories, not one of the tales that follow has roots in the tragedy of Katrina.

I had a conversation with a waitress in a Decatur Street restaurant during a visit to New Orleans in the spring before Katrina. During my mammoth muffeletta lunch, it came out that I was in the city doing research for this book. Between mouthfuls, I asked her if she believed in ghosts and was surprised at how quickly she responded.

"Of *course* I believe in ghosts. It's hard to live in this city and *not* believe in them." She said that almost every building in the French Quarter had a ghost story, and even if it didn't, you couldn't help but *feel* the dead trying to whisper their stories to you as you walked by.

That said, she did not like the way New Orleans' ghost stories were being told—both by the operators of the ghost tours and by the writers who cast the accounts in similarly sensational overtones. She believed in ghosts, but did not appreciate the way their tragedies were made into entertainment. At the time, this woman might have seemed too sensitive, seeing as how most of the city's established paranormal legends went back well over a century. But now, in the aftermath of Katrina, it is likely that many people would agree. Some of New Orleans' tragedies ought not be told.

What follows are the true—or purportedly true—ghost stories of Louisiana, from the crowded streets of the Vieux Carre to the far-flung swamps and bayous of more remote communities. Almost all the folklore emanates from the 19th century, although all stories based on first-hand accounts come from interviews that took place in early 2005. And although I hope these stories do, for the most part, entertain, despite the misgivings of a certain waitress, I have also been careful to respect the recent tragedies New Orleans has suffered.

Now turn the page. The spirits and legends of one of the United States' most captivating regions are waiting. There are ghosts stories to be read.

1

Plantation Phantoms and Haunted Houses

The Ghosts of the Myrtles Plantation

Given the incredible amount of supernatural phenomena that occur on this St. Francisville plantation, it might be said that ghosts don't so much haunt the Myrtles Plantation as *populate* it. Indeed, a visitor can scarcely take a step through the doors of the grand old house without the possibility of coming face-to-face with one of the plantation's many spirits. They are said to exist in practically every room, down every hall, under the furniture, on the stairs, in the mirrors and around each corner. The manifold accounts of the restless dead have made the Myrtles famous—or perhaps infamous. There are few places in the world with histories as dark and as tragic as the plantation house. Over course of its 200-plus years, no fewer than nine untimely deaths have occurred within its walls.

It seems that the home was destined for notoriety from the very beginning, in 1796, when Revolutionary War General David Bradford decided to build there. Some versions of the legend tell us that when he first rode onto the property, Bradford saw an apparition drifting among the trees—a shimmering outline of a lone Indian girl, lingering for a few seconds before vanishing within the wooded shadows. It's impossible to know whether or not he was aware of it, but his chosen site of construction is said to be right on top of a Tunica Indian burial ground. Did the girl appear to warn Bradford against building there? If so, the general couldn't have been too rattled. He went ahead with his plans, erecting his four-room cottage on hallowed ground. According to all accounts, Bradford himself lived and died there peacefully, suffering none of the mortal misfortune that would come to mark the place. His daughter and granddaughters, however, would not be so lucky.

Sara Matilda inherited the Myrtles Plantation from her father in 1818 and married Judge Clarke Woodruff soon after. The first years for the Woodruff family were prosperous. Sara gave birth to three blonde-haired daughters, and their plantation thrived, with over 500 slaves working the surrounding cotton and indigo fields, and another 40 household slaves taking care of the Woodruff's domestic affairs. Yet even as the Woodruffs grew wealthy off the blood and sweat of their servants, the seed of their destruction had already been planted.

Judge Clarke Woodruff had a wandering eye and, like so many Southern patricians of his day, availed himself of his female slaves. His favorite was a household slave named Chloe. She was a young woman, sharp and ambitious and all too ready to use her charms to move up in the household hierarchy. Equating information with power, Chloe took advantage of her relationship with the judge to learn as much as she could about the goings-on in the plantation, constantly grilling him with questions whenever they had time alone.

Woodruff was glad to oblige his mistress, at least while he was still interested in her. Unfortunately for Chloe, though, the judge didn't remain interested for long. Tired of Chloe, he began to lavish his attention on other female slaves. In a short while, Woodruff stopped acknowledging Chloe altogether, and the ambitious household slave found herself cut off from her one source of influence among the other slaves in the house. But Chloe's ambitions wouldn't be thwarted so easily.

No longer able to get information from Woodruff directly, she started eavesdropping on the judge's personal conversations, getting what information she could through doors and keyholes, behind curtains, in closets. Her former relationship with the judge made her bold, and she took big chances, assuming that even if she were caught, she'd only suffer a slap on the wrist. She couldn't imagine the judge treating her harshly. If only she knew how wrong she was.

Chloe was caught one day, leaning a bit too close against a door that was open a bit too wide. Woodruff was hosting a meeting with a group of fellow planters, one of whom spotted the eavesdropping slave and pointed her out. The judge was as embarrassed as he was angry, and he ordered the harsh penalty then and there. For her curiosity, Chloe was to have her left ear cut off and be cast out of the plantation house to the brutal work in the field.

Thus Chloe, the once-pampered mistress of Myrtles Plantation, now worked out in the field, sweating it out, day after backbreaking day, a green turban tied around her head to conceal the gaping wound that once was her left ear. And yet she was determined that her story would not end there. Her ambitions were far too lofty to see her meet an eventless end among anonymous field hands in the heart of the Deep South. No, Chloe would not be treated this way.

Her opportunity came during one of the judge's daughters' birthdays. During the bustle of preparations, she sneaked into the kitchen with her own little gift for the birthday girl—a white cake baked with a secret, potentially lethal ingredient: oleander leaf. No one can say for certain what

Ghosts don't so much haunt Myrtles Plantation as populate it.

Chloe's intentions were, for the oleander leaf isn't always deadly. If ingested in small doses, it only causes illness, not death. Some have suggested that Chloe wasn't interested in revenge, but was just looking to win back her place in the household. If she added just enough oleander so that Woodruff's daughter would become ill, Chloe would be able to effectively nurse the daughter back to health, and thus win back her place in the Myrtles. This may have been the plan. But given the tragic outcome, we will probably never know.

Not long after the party, Sara Matilda fell ill, along with two of her daughters. The three Woodruffs were in agony, writhing in bedridden anguish, tended to by doctors who had no idea what to make of their condition. Moved by either guilt or ambition, Chloe stepped forward, stating that she was able to help. She tried, tirelessly administering to the trio throughout the day, but all of her efforts ended up being futile. If she had indeed planned to save them, then she'd made a mistake and given them too much poison. And if revenge was what she was initially after, then no amount of nursing would succeed in alleviating her guilty conscience. They'd ingested lethal amounts of Chloe's poison and died that night.

Judge Woodruff, beside himself with grief, retreated to his room. No one suspected Chloe for the deaths, and she was free to head back to her own quarters among the field hands. Her scheme had backfired. Whether her actions had been motivated by vengeance or vindication, she was not prepared for the terrible guilt that washed over her. The deaths of the two girls and their mother were all she could think about. She'd been by their bedsides at the very end, had witnessed their last tortured moments and was instantly appalled at what she'd done.

In an effort to unburden her conscience, Chloe turned to her fellow slaves and told them what she'd done. But if she was hoping for any sort of clemency from her peers, she was gravely mistaken. Shocked by her actions and horrified at what Judge Woodruff might do if he found them harboring the woman who killed his wife and two of his daughters, the slaves took immediate action. They dragged Chloe out to a large oak tree on the plantation, slung a noose over one of the branches and hanged her. And so Chloe was the fourth woman to die on the plantation that day.

Everything at the Myrtles Plantation changed after that. The cheer and prosperity that marked the Woodruffs' first few years was snuffed out as an unsettling darkness descended over the property. A feeling of dread grew in the shadows of the oak trees and crape myrtles. Slaves and planters alike began to avoid walking the grounds alone. Strange visions were spotted—Chloe in her green turban, staring blankly at startled witnesses, there one moment, gone the next. Others claimed to hear footfalls through the trees, whispers in the dusk.

The situation in the plantation house was no better. Cries were heard in the middle of the night. More than one servant claimed to see the two blonde-haired sisters chasing one another through the house. There were cold spots in the middle of summer, invisible hands tugging at garments and the sound of sad weeping. There were also the blood-chilling sightings of Chloe, standing tall, staring ahead blankly for several moments before vanishing into midair. And then there was the large, ornate mirror in the front hall.

On all plantations across the South, it was common practice to cover every mirror with black cloth whenever a death occurred in the house. This was to allay a popular superstition that mirrors were able to absorb the spirits of the recently deceased, cursing them to an eternity within the houses they died in. Yet in the grief and confusion following the deaths in the plantation, no one thought to cover the mirror in the front hall. Ever since, the mirror has taken a central place among the numerous phenomena in the Myrtles.

While the ghosts of the three poisoned Woodruffs are said to wander throughout the house, it is believed that they always end up converging within the gilded frame of the great mirror. Household servants attested to this early on, pointing to the bizarre patterns that spontaneously appeared in the glass. Dark discolorations resembling handprints appeared in the mirror mere days after the three

Woodruffs were buried. The shapes in the mirror were always shifting, appearing in one corner one day, vanishing in the evening, only to appear in another part of the mirror the next morning.

The near eradication of his family, combined with all the strange manifestations in his home, was too much for Clarke Woodruff. With his one surviving daughter, the judge moved to New Orleans, entrusting the care of his plantation to one of his caretakers. Nothing more was written of the Woodruff ghosts on the Myrtles Plantation until the property was sold to the Ruffin Stirling family in 1834.

Well aware of the house's ugly history, the Stirlings financed dramatic renovations before settling in. They added an entire wing to the house, sparing no expense on lavish adornment. Crystal chandeliers, intricate ironwork, French furnishings, marble mantelpieces—the Myrtles was turned into one of Louisiana's finest plantations. On top of the huge additions, the Stirlings were particular about small details that were designed to protect the new owners from the house's cursed legacy.

The Stirlings installed locks upside down with the belief that this would confuse wandering spirits. Along the front and back porches, they added stained glass windows painted over with crucifixes. And if this wasn't enough to ward off evil, they had the likenesses of cherubs built into the chandelier in one of the bedchambers to discourage supernatural mischief. They had the images of nuns' heads carved into the decorative medallions that adorned the walls. Yet despite all these precautions, the Stirlings weren't able to avoid the ill fortune that had so scarred their predecessors.

Not that all the Stirlings' difficulties could be blamed on the spirits in the house. The Civil War broke out when the Stirlings resided in the Myrtles. They were a large family, with eight sons and one daughter, and there were few households who sacrificed so much for the Southern cause. Most of the sons went to fight for the Confederacy, and every Stirling who donned a gray uniform to face the Union fell in battle. The eldest son, Louis, didn't go to war but was killed in the gaming room over a gambling debt.

One of the Stirling sons managed to dodge an untimely death, but the Myrtle Plantation was bequeathed to Sara, the only daughter, who married a local attorney named William Winters. They had one child, a girl, who lived to her third year and then died of yellow fever in 1861. In 1871, a lone rider appeared at the front door of the plantation house, calling for Sara's husband. Winters walked out to the front porch to answer the visitor and found himself face-to-face with a shotgun-wielding man who instantly pulled the trigger. Reeling backwards with a hole in his chest, Winters fell into the house, staggering up the stairs to his wife. He managed to make it to the 17th step before collapsing in a bloody heap. Sara never recovered from the sight of her dead husband. She locked herself in her bedroom, where she spent the remainder of her days in silence, creaking back and forth in a rocking chair.

One last untimely death occurred on the grounds of the Myrtles Plantation in 1927. The story goes that a caretaker was shot to death during an attempted robbery, gunned down just outside his cottage. The murderers were never caught, and no one can say what they were after. This was the last in the chain of brutal episodes that mark the Myrtles' history. But the plantation's murderous chronicle does not end here.

Today, the Myrtles Plantation is a bed-and-breakfast and popular tourist attraction. Placed on the National Park Service's Register of Historic Places, it draws many visitors interested in seeing a remarkably well-preserved piece of America's antebellum South. But history buffs aren't the only ones attracted to the Myrtles. The plantation is largely regarded as one of the country's most haunted houses, setting an unofficial record for the number of ghostly phenomena that occur within its grounds. Thus in addition to history buffs, the Myrtles Plantation also receives its fair share of paranormal buffs.

When the current proprietors, John and Teeta Moss, purchased the plantation, neither was too interested in its ghostly legends. Unwilling to compromise the Myrtles' official designation as a historic site, the Mosses made firm rules against visitors conducting paranormal investigations. Both were skeptical about the ghost stories and planned on concentrating on the plantation's history rather than its legends.

Yet it wasn't long before their experiences in the plantation imbued them with an appreciation for its ghost stories. Regardless of the Mosses' skepticism and rules against paranormal investigations, stories of ghostly activity in the house continued to thrive. Visitors to the bed-and-breakfast frequently claimed all sorts of bizarre experiences.

They talked about waking up in the middle of the night to see a black woman in a green turban staring blankly at them. Standing there just long enough for witnesses to shake off sleep, the figure, which could only have been Chloe, would then suddenly blink out of sight, leaving the startled guests staring into the darkness. Some claimed to hear the sound of a rocking chair creaking in their room, together with a woman's faint, discordant humming. Often two little girls could be heard giggling in the darkness, their footsteps running through the halls and rooms in the middle of the night. On other occasions, guests claimed to hear painful cries coming from the Ruffin-Stirling Room, where the two Woodruff girls were poisoned nearly 200 years ago.

Specific phenomena are constantly reported in certain places. For instance, only those staying in the Judge Clarke Woodruff Suite hear heavy staggering footfalls making their way up the stairs outside the suite. The footsteps, growing more sluggish as they proceed upwards, always stop at the same place—on the 17th step. Of course, this is the precise spot where William Winter collapsed after he was shot in the chest.

Occasionally, rattled visitors staying in the Fannie Williamson Room will complain about an extreme cold that suddenly descends over the chamber. This cold is sometimes accompanied by an ominous feeling, as though there is someone or some*thing* in the room not at all happy about sharing it. Many of those who have tried to oblige the presence in the room by leaving are often dismayed to find the door momentarily stuck, as though barred from the outside. Though no one has been trapped in the freezing room for more than several seconds, the experience is often creepy enough to make guests ask for another suite.

Guests who book the caretaker's cottage also find themselves encountering a spirit of the Myrtles Plantation's past. It seems that the man who was killed thwarting the 1927 robbery has taken it upon himself to keep up with his duties.

The caretaker must have been an early riser, for he's only ever spotted in the morning. Some days, around sunrise, he is seen on the surrounding grounds, faintly transparent and dressed in faded overalls, slowly trudging from the cottage toward the plantation house. Other guests have been woken in the small hours of the morning by slow and steady footsteps on the main floor, along with the sound and smell of food sizzling on a frying pan. Early morning investigations of the cottage always yield the same results—nothing but empty rooms in the dimness of the day's first light.

Patrons of the bed-and-breakfast aren't the only ones to have run-ins with the spirits of the Myrtles Plantation. The employees and proprietors have their share of encounters as well. One tour guide, Hester Eby, has gone on record about the things she's experienced while guiding people through the plantation house. Over the years, she's heard girls giggling in empty rooms, small voices whispering back and forth and doors locking and unlocking on their own.

In her book, *The Haunting of Louisiana*, Barbara Sillery relates Hester's most dramatic supernatural experience. According to Sillery's account, it was eight o'clock in the morning, and Hester was the first employee to arrive that day. She had just begun her opening duties when she heard a car approaching—the first visitors of the day. Stepping out onto the front porch, she saw three people in the vehicle: a man and woman in the front and a little girl with bright blonde hair sitting in the back. Hester went back inside as they parked their car and got out, the man and woman in front, the little girl skipping along behind her parents. She was finishing up the last of her opening duties as the family stepped into the gift shop.

Or rather, not quite the entire family. Hester noted that only two of them, the man and the woman, appeared at the door. The blonde-haired girl was not with them. It didn't strike her as strange at first; the girl could've been out on the porch playing with the nanny doll that rested on a stool. Not until the woman asked for two adult tickets for entry into the house did Hester inquire about their daughter. Wasn't she going to come in as well?

The woman stared at her for a long moment, confused. She didn't know what Ester was talking about—it was just she and her husband. Ester was sure of what she had seen and didn't know what to make of the woman standing in front of her, feigning ignorance over the little passenger in the back seat of the car, who had skipped up to the house. Still, she was an employee of the plantation and her job was to sell tickets, so she took the money and handed the visitors their vouchers, waiting until the couple had walked through before going out to take a look.

Much to her surprise, there was nobody on the front porch; the nanny doll by the door was untouched. She looked over the parking lot and even stole a quick glance into the couple's car. Nobody. There was no trace of the girl she had seen just minutes ago. Only when she turned around and began walking to the plantation house did it hit her. She looked up at the ancient building and felt as if the windows were staring back at her. Of course—she'd just seen one of the Woodruff girls.

Hester is adamant about what she saw: "She had long blonde hair and a black and white dress complete with pantaloons. She was about eight or nine years old...the same age as the oldest daughter of the Woodruffs when she died from eating too much poisoned birthday cake." In all her years working at the Myrtles, after hearing all the little giggles and whispers, Hester Eby had finally laid eyes on one of the little ghosts that she is convinced haunts her workplace.

She isn't the only one who has caught a glimpse of a Woodruff girl. In fact, a good many people who've taken photographs of the great mirror in the entrance hall, the same one that was left uncovered so many years ago, swear that they've captured vague images of people in the reflection. Various photographs have yielded different results— one, a woman standing on a staircase; another, two small people, presumably girls; yet another, an eerie resemblance to a woman's face pressed against glass.

Indeed, the mirror in the front hall is one of the main attractions for paranormal enthusiasts, and not just for the images that often appear in photographs. The dark discolorations on the glass, which resemble small handprints, have been there for as long as anyone can remember. This is odd, for while the frame that hangs in the house today is the same one that was there when the poisoned Woodruffs were buried, the actual mirror has been changed numerous times. Yet each time, with every new glass, the discolored marks have appeared within a matter of days. The Mosses witnessed this phenomenon themselves when they saw the dark markings appear after putting in a new mirror about a decade ago. Could the markings be from small invisible hands pressing out from the other side? Incredible as it sounds, more than one former skeptic has come away from the Myrtles Plantation entertaining this possibility.

There is no better example than Teeta Moss. When she and her husband first moved into the Myrtles, they gave little thought to all the ghost stories that circulated about the place. *Just publicity*, Teeta thought, publicity that she had no interest in pursuing herself.

Today, however, her opinion on this matter has changed. After years of living on the plantation, seeing the things she has seen and hearing, firsthand, the innumerable accounts from her wonderstruck guests, she can no longer be so certain. And so she has continued to foster the public fascination with the ghosts of her home. On Friday and Saturday nights, guests of the plantation can take part in "mystery tours," during which enthusiasts are guided through the antebellum plantation's haunted past—a past which visitors might find staring them in the face, if any one of the house's many spirits are feeling at all active that night.

The Haunted House

True, the title might seem too general, but if you were to approach any New Orleans resident who knows his or her city and ask, "Which way to the haunted house?" there's a good chance you'd be directed to the enormous three-story building on the corner of Royal Street and Governor Nicholl Street. As opulent as it is imposing, LaLaurie Mansion has inspired a legend that is easily among the most famous folk tales in the French Quarter, if not the entire state.

Her name was Delphine LaLaurie. She was one of the city's privileged, a Creole woman of the Vieux Carre graced with an exceptional talent for good living. She and her husband, Dr. Louis LaLaurie, moved into the mansion on 1140 Royal Street in 1832, and almost as soon as they arrived, Madame LaLaurie went about making sure that they were the most envied family in town.

She strove for nothing less than perfection. With her impeccable looks, her bewildering wardrobe of the finest French fashions, her charming and well-mannered children and her wealthy and intelligent husband, it was impossible to find fault in anything LaLaurie put her hands on. And just in case her flawlessness was lost on her peers, even after all this, there were her parties.

No one threw a party like Madame LaLaurie. For the short time her family resided in the mansion, her weekend soirées were *the* elite social occasions. It was during these gatherings that the lady of the house showered her guests with undeniable proof of her excellence. She could be called New Orleans' antebellum Martha Stewart. There was a limitless supply of the finest wines served in the best crystal. The food was served on European china. The floor was adorned with exotic, foreign rugs. And of course, there was Madame LaLaurie herself, making her rounds among her guests, oozing easy charm, virtually glowing in some silk gown, not a single, sleek hair out of place.

Yet as impressive as the LaLaurie luxuries often were to revelers, there were a few among her guests who perceived something beyond the glittering appearances. Part of it had to do with the demeanor of the household slaves. While few slaves across the South would have been known for their self-assurance in the presence of their masters, the meekness of the LaLaurie slaves bordered on socially awkward. They never made eye contact with the guests, and their hands shook when they doled out servings from their platters. Under their well-kept uniforms, they were far too thin, stooped and emaciated, half-starved. And when they stole sidelong glances at Madame LaLaurie, pure terror would momentarliy flash in their eyes.

Perceptive guests noticed something else as well. Sometimes, when Madame LaLaurie's gaze fell on one of her slaves, the look of easy kindness she always wore would suddenly crack into a blood-chilling expression of absolute hate. This flicker of red-hot cruelty never lasted for more than a second or two, but it never failed to startle those who noticed it. These guests always walked away with the impression that they had caught a glimpse through a window into Madame LaLaurie's heart, and they had seen, for a mere instant, a soul of pure evil.

Yet these were just momentary glances and quickly passing impressions. In the blink of an eye, Madame LaLaurie would be back to normal, with her brilliant smile and her

Cries of tortured slaves could still be heard from within the LaLaurie Mansion long after it had been abandoned.

smooth social graces, causing witnesses to wonder if they had actually seen what they thought they had seen. Week after week, the LaLaurie Mansion was packed with the most distinguished of New Orleans society. The parties were perfect, and the LaLauries' reputation was unimpeachable.

That changed late on a dark night, when a terrified high-pitched scream shattered the silence hanging over Royal and Governor Nicholl Streets. According to the legend, the shriek was loud enough to get one of the LaLauries' neighbors out of bed. Peering from his bedroom window across the street at the looming mansion, the man witnessed a startling sight in one of the mansion's windows. There he saw none other than the ever-graceful Delphine LaLaurie in a dimly lit room with a whip raised high, standing over a slave girl who couldn't have been more than eight years old. The light was on in the room where the struggle was occurring, and the man had a clear view of what was going on. The girl was lashed under LaLaurie's whip, then managed to get away, running up to the third floor with the mistress of the house right behind her. He watched the struggle repeat itself in the room behind another window, as the girl evaded several blows and made her escape again, this time onto the roof of the mansion. Madame LaLaurie followed her up even to the roof, her tall figure moving quickly and silently after the child, whip raised over her head. The man watched as the girl quickly ran out of room to maneuver until she was cornered against the edge of the building with LaLaurie standing in front of her and nowhere to go except down. All the man could do was watch in horror as the girl turned and jumped off the roof, landing unseen in the LaLaurie courtyard below. He knew there was no way she could have survived the fall.

The next day, the man informed the authorities about what he had seen. Yet while there were laws against cruelty to slaves, they were often ignored in the antebellum South—especially when the accused was as respected as Delphine LaLaurie. Still, this isn't to say that LaLaurie's brutal crime went without consequences. For while the authorities were reluctant to press the matter, LaLaurie soon found herself coming under scrutiny from the people she once considered friends.

Chasing one's eight-year-old slave up onto the roof of one's house and forcing the poor child to jump was hardly considered dignified behavior. Fewer and fewer of the city's elite showed up to LaLaurie's parties, and the ones who did attend began paying close attention to the state of her house-hold slaves. That was when the rumors began to fly.

Guests noticed all sorts of troubling details that they had previously overlooked. Not only were LaLaurie's slaves obviously malnourished and in a near-constant state of barely restrained terror, but many of them bore visible wounds. Granted, these wounds were only just visible—the tip of an ugly gash poking out from under the edge of one man's collar, burn scars on another's palms, a woman doing her tortured best to conceal a limp. Yet as LaLaurie's guests started paying less attention to their affluent surroundings and more attention to the people who were serving them, it became obvious that there was something very wrong. All the social graces in the world couldn't save Madame LaLaurie from the growing society gossip. As her popularity plummeted, speculation emerged concering what was going on behind the mansion's closed doors. The rumors spread from affluent circles to the general population. Soon, it seemed like the entire city was whispering about the sadistic mistress LaLaurie. All sorts of ugly theories abounded, but even the most sordid among them didn't prepare the city for the evil that was festering within those walls.

On April 10, 1834, the mansion caught fire. No one can say with any certainty how the fire started. Some have theorized that it was an arsonist sympathetic to the slaves. Others thought that it was one of the slaves—LaLaurie's cook, specifically—who, because he couldn't face another moment in that cursed house, set fire to the kitchen. Whatever the case, the fire spread quickly, and it wasn't long before the flames and the smoke drew the community around the mansion.

People showed up from all corners of the city, buckets in hand, ready to fight the fire before it spread.

Delphine LaLaurie was there in the thick of it, directing the volunteers so as to minimize the damage, making sure that her most valued possessions were being moved from harm's way. Amid the chaos of the conflagration, Madame LaLaurie was as cool and graceful as ever. Then one of the volunteers asked her about the slaves. Where were they? Were they safe from the blaze that was still spreading through her home?

LaLaurie's cool façade instantly crumbled into a vile expression. Fire reflected in her eyes as she glared at the man. "It would be in your best interest to mind your own business," LaLaurie snapped. "I will do what I will with my property."

Nevertheless, the fire-fighting effort had gone beyond her control. Led by a local official named Judge Canongo, the volunteers were pushing on to the third floor, clearing out rooms and putting out fires as they went. Their advance was halted by a heavy wooden door that led to the attic. Aware of the rumors of the LaLaurie slaves, Canongo was preoccupied with what had become of them. By the time they were nearing the top floor, he had been in practically every room in the mansion and had seen almost no household servants. The only place left where they could be, he knew, was beyond the garret door. Fearing the fire may have claimed them, Canongo looked to Doctor LaLaurie, who had been accompanying the volunteers, and ordered him to unlock the door. When the doctor flat-out refused, Canongo acted, ordering a handful of volunteers to break it down. In their worse nightmares, neither he nor any of the men with him could have imagined what lay beyond.

There, in the smoky attic, were the LaLaurie slaves—more than a dozen bound men and women, either chained to the walls with heavy steel manacles, tied down upon tabletops or imprisoned in cages. Many of those on the tables were dead, having succumbed to horrifying torture, their cold faces frozen in terror. Some lay disemboweled, their intestines pulled out and wrapped around their abdomens. Others had their mouths and eyes sewn shut. More than one was completely dismembered, slumped against a wall without any limbs, in plain view of their shorn arm and legs. One woman had been crammed into a tiny cage after her limbs had been broken; her bones had set awkwardly, causing her appendages to jut out from the cage at brutal angles. Other details are too terrible to relate in these pages. The volunteers standing at the doorway reeled back in horror, retching at the unbelievable sight and the smell of rot. Even Dr. LaLaurie, who had never guessed the extent of his wife's madness, blanched and turned away.

In mute shock, the firefighters stumbled out of the LaLaurie Mansion. The blaze in the house had been put out, but the flames of public indignation were about to rage out of control. It began when the doctors arrived. By this time, a big crowd of bystanders had gathered around the house. And their fury was palpable when the mutilated bodies were brought down from the attic and carried into waiting carriages.

Madame LaLaurie got out of New Orleans the very next day, and even that almost wasn't quick enough. After locking herself in the fire-gutted mansion the moment her tortured slaves were led through the shocked crowd, she and her husband immediately packed up what valuables they could carry. By the time the sun came up on April 11, word had spread through town about Delphine LaLaurie's perverse pastime. A gang of angry citizens gathered around her home.

The crowd grew with each passing hour, as did its fury, and by the afternoon, it had become an angry mob, shouting insults at the walls, hurling bricks through windows, demanding vengeance. Just when it seemed things were going to get out of control, the courtyard gates burst open and a heavy carriage came barreling out, cutting a passage through the crowd. Inside were Madame LaLaurie and her husband. They rode straight through the Vieux Carre and out of town, never to return.

The mob outside cut loose, storming into the mansion and destroying everything in its path. Furniture was thrown through windows onto the streets below. Pianos were lit aflame, mattresses gutted, windows smashed. If a cordon of police hadn't showed up when it did, it's likely the mob would've razed the LaLaurie Mansion to the ground that day.

While Delphine LaLaurie moved on—the most popular theory finds her settling with her family in Paris, France—the stain of her of evil remained on 1140 Royal Street. And for many years, it seemed that no amount of remodeling and renovation could remove it. Almost immediately after the LaLauries fled, the mansion's doors were barred and sealed, and it remained unoccupied for years. No one would look at the mansion the same way again. Once a vaunted symbol of Creole aristocracy, it had become a monument of evil, a looming reminder of humanity's worst behavior. And inside, something unnatural was coming to life.

For some, all it took was a glance to know that the mansion had become possessed by something. Others couldn't bear to walk in its looming shadow; they crossed the street and averted their eyes when they walked by. Yet for those living in the vicinity, it was all too obvious that the LaLaurie Mansion was a haunted building, scarred by atrocities that none dared to imagine.

It is said that the eerie sights and sounds began almost as soon as the mansion was vacated. Neighbors would be woken in the middle of the night by the sound of agonized screams coming from within. On other nights, lights would be seen flashing and flickering within, and shadows would move across the windows. One mangled face with a tortured expression was repeatedly seen gazing out of one of the windows. And then there were also the frequent sightings of the little slave girl running back and forth upon the roof, disappearing after she jumped off the edge. Only a few desperate people dared venture into the LaLaurie Mansion during this period—two or three homeless people who needed roofs over their heads for a night. It was said that none of them were seen again.

Years passed, and the public outrage over Madame LaLaurie's deeds slowly faded, but strange goings-on continued to plague the mansion. In 1837, three years after the fire, LaLaurie's agent finally managed to sell the building. The new owner, however, did not last. He was tormented by all sorts of strange sounds coming from the attic, and more than once he spied a limping apparition making its way through his halls. And then there was the little black girl. Terrified of some assailant the man was unable to see, she ran pell-mell through the house, her footsteps often startling him awake. Yet every time he laid eyes on the girl, she only remained visible for a few short seconds, and vanished the moment her foot touched the stairs. The man only lasted a few months living under such conditions, and he tried leasing out the rooms after he moved out. But his tenants weren't able to put up with the strange goings-on either, and the building was soon abandoned once more.

In a sense, this summarized much of the mansion's history since the 1834 fire. The mansion passed through many hands, used at different times as an integrated school, dance academy, single residence and apartment building. All the while, there were the reports of weird happenings, whispers of its ugly past.

Between owners, the mansion was often unoccupied, sometimes lying abandoned for years. But despite all the years and all the different owners, the LaLaurie Mansion would never shed its tragic history, or its haunted reputation. The event that rocked the community so many years ago has passed from history to become one of New Orleans' most publicized legends. Every night, several groups of tourists on formal ghost walks are led to 1140 Royal Street, where supernatural interpreters tell the story of its brutal and haunted past.

Today, it seems as if the tortured spirits of the mansion have finally moved on. The building underwent extensive work in 1976 and 1980, and was restored, renovated and converted into luxury apartments. Over the doorbell hangs a sign that reads: "Private Residence. No tours." So it is that the doors of the LaLaurie Mansion are once again locked against curious outsiders. And despite the continued attention the mansion receives from the paranormal enthusiasts who crowd nightly around its walls, its residents value their privacy and have kept mum about whatever does or does not continue to occur inside.

The Singing in the Attic

The guards at Griffon House had never seen a pair of more patriotic soldiers. The two men had been imprisoned within the stately New Orleans home for nearly a week. From the moment they arrived they did not let up on the military songs, bellowing jingoistic Union Army tunes at the top of their lungs, their voices carrying from the top floor to the basement, to the pedestrians down the block. One of their favorites was "John Brown's Body." They stayed up late into the night, every night, hollering the "Glory Glory Hallelujah" chorus with such zeal that they quickly won the hearts of the men who guarded them. Their sympathetic captors, ashamed that two such upstanding soldiers were held under lock and key, started sneaking whiskey to their two jailed comrades, and the strains of "John Brown's Body" were soon infused with drunken enthusiasm.

It was early May 1862, and the Union Army under General Benjamin Butler had just occupied New Orleans. The general put the burg under heavy martial law, imposing a harsh and uncompromising order over the city, and the reviled bluecoats were stationed on practically every street corner, glowering in the hot southern sun, waiting for an excuse to throw someone in the stockades. The occupation would be remembered as one of the darker periods in New Orleans' history, when injustice abounded and the city's prisons were filled to bursting.

A good number of prominent houses were converted into prisons to accommodate the sudden swell of convicts. Griffon House was owned by a New Orleans socialite named Adam Griffon who fled the city just as General Butler's

General Benjamin Butler

troops were marching in. His luxurious mansion was promptly turned into a stockade by the occupying army, and the two men locked up in the attic were among the first to be incarcerated there. They were in for looting, arrested just after Butler had passed his severe ordinance against theft. Their detainment seemed especially tragic to the guards in Griffon House. For while they may have been guilty of theft, the pair's boisterous display of northern gallantry, sung out loud all hours of the day, made them ideal fighting men for the Union cause. Or so they thought. In actuality, the prisoners' show of patriotism was a show of deception.

The two men imprisoned on the top floor of Griffon House were actually Confederate soldiers who deserted after the fighting at Fort Jackson in late April. They had been making their way through New Orleans disguised as Union officers when they were apprehended for stealing from a local merchant. Terrified that they might be found out as Confederate deserters—or even worse, mistaken for Confederate spies—the pair made sure to put on such a show of northern bravado that there would be no doubt of their allegiances. It turned out their act was so convincing that their alleged comrades took a very real liking to them and began sneaking them whiskey to help pass the time.

If the two deserters were encouraged at the success of their deception, they would soon wallow in the futility of it when they learned that Butler ordered that any man caught looting be shot, regardless of what side he was on, Union or Confederate. Suddenly, the pair's charade was rendered pointless, and the two Southerners became obsessed with the idea of their imminent execution. It seems, however, that their execution wasn't imminent enough.

The city of New Orleans was still in turmoil in the wake of the takeover, and the Union soldiers were too occupied with other matters to put two petty criminals to death. Far from being elated at being granted this extra time, the Confederates-in-disguise greeted each new day with more dread than the day before, unable to bear the thought of waiting another day for their inevitable end. Finally, they decided to take matters into their own hands. They bribed one of their guards to sneak two pistols into their cell. One night about a week after they were arrested, the two men lay side-by-side on one of the beds, pressed the barrels of their guns to each other's heart and, at the count of three, shot each other at the same time. Both died instantly.

The gruesome scene that greeted the guards the next morning made the two dead captives into celebrity casualties of General Butler, and it wasn't long before their true identities were found out. While this intrigue only added to the two dead men's popularity, it wasn't their tragic end alone that made the story of the double suicide in Griffon House into one of New Orleans' most lasting Civil War legends.

Things would never be the same in Griffon House. Anyone who spent any time in the resplendent old home after the Civil War talked about the strange things that went on in the attic. Over the years, ownership of the house changed frequently, and it was used for many different purposes. But whether it was a factory, personal residence or boarding house, the stories never varied much.

The earliest accounts of the phenomenon in Griffon House came from frightened witnesses who heard noises in the attic. These stories were told by the first workers who were employed at Griffon House after it was converted into a lamp factory shortly after the war. Men and women working late into the night spoke of the creaking footsteps plodding across the attic above them, and of the sound of heavy chains being dragged behind. More than one employee at the factory would venture up into garret to see who was making the sounds, but no one ever found a soul in the attic. There was only a darkened room and a strange sense of foreboding that deterred anyone from staying there long. But the strange goings-on didn't stop there. Even as word spread of the footsteps in the attic, employees at Griffon House became privy to stranger, more frightening events.The voices began a few days after the footsteps. The first people who heard them might have assumed two drunken employees had made their way up to the top floor. Raucous laughter drifted down from the attic, along with faint strains of song. Yet anyone who went up to the attic to investigate only found the same deserted room, dark and still as a tomb. The singing continued, night after night, growing more and more pronounced, until witnesses were able to make out the words of "John Brown's Body."

By this time, most people believed the incidents on Griffon House's top floor were linked to the two men who had killed themselves there. Not only were the disembodied voices obviously singing the same song the deserters had sung during their incarceration, but more than one pedestrian walking by the house at night claimed to see two pale men dressed in Union uniforms staring out from the attic window. It is said that no one who caught sight of these ashen faces believed they were looking at living men. Some onlookers experienced a jolt of panic when their eyes took in the two men at the window, and they were possessed by the sudden urge to run as far away as they could. Others found themselves staring agape at the faces, overcome with sense of terrible awe, comprehending on some level that they were witnessing some sort of manifestation of death itself—that they were staring at a reflection of the fate that awaited them all.

If the two dead soldiers in Griffon House attic became a symbol of mortality for a small number of New Orleans residents, the persistent sightings of the ghosts over succeeding generations also made them into one of the Crescent City's most enduring legends. Indeed, given the accounts of people's experiences in Griffon House over the years, it seems as if the spirits there have grown more active, and more famous, with each passing decade. While early reports were limited to the sounds of song, chains and footsteps from within, and sightings of the two through the attic window from the outside, later stories were far more chilling.

Griffon House continued to be used as a factory through much of the early 1900s, and the people who had most of the run-ins with the house's spirits were employees working the late shift. The employees had largely gotten used to the occasional singing and stomping around in the attic, and they learned to accept the supernatural phenomena with surprising nonchalance. But then the ghosts changed their habits.

It began when the footsteps moved on to the stairs—big, unnatural, footfalls that boomed through the house with every step, like some giant of a man was lumbering down the stairs. The footsteps never made it to the base of the stairs; they always stopped just before reaching the last step. Yet the moment the sound of the thunderous descent abated, the phantom voices that were so often heard in the attic struck up the chorus of "John Brown's Body." This time, however, the drunken pair seemed to be much closer, their disharmonious singing loud and clear, as if they were standing right next to startled witnesses.

Soon after they ventured down the stairs, the spirits took up the habit of tossing things around. More than one late-night worker stared in horrified fascination as a chair suddenly flew across a room, as if hurled by some angry invisible force. Sometimes this force acted with incredible strength, tearing fixtures from walls and hurtling them great distances down Griffon's halls. On occasion, this phenomenon resulted in near-fatal consequences when objects just narrowly missed witnesses who had to dodge out of the way of a flying table, chair or chandelier.

Indeed, there is evidence that the ghostly pair has grown angrier with the passing years. While some people in Griffon House were being attacked by flying objects, others began to talk of sudden temperature drops in the house, which caused individuals to shiver in the middle of sweltering New Orleans summers. There were other accounts of invisible hands that would sporadically grab and shove people as they walked through the home.

The most famous incident said to have occurred in Griffon House took place sometime in the 1950s, when the old home was converted into a boarding house. An elderly female resident was awakened from a nap by the feeling of something dripping on her forearm. She opened her eyes in groggy curiosity and was instantly startled awake at the sight of her bleeding arm. Assuming that she was cut, the woman wiped the blood off her skin to get a better look at the wound. But her skin was unmarked; there was no trace of a gash. She was staring in confusion at the smear of blood when another drop fell onto her arm. That was when she looked up.

In the next moment, she was running screaming from her room, garbling in near-unintelligible panic about the "bleeding house." The landlord was in her room investigating within the hour. Sure enough, when he looked up, he saw the same thing that had sent his tenant running in terror. A section of the ceiling looked like a saturated smear of blood that fell, one drop at a time, right next to the woman's armchair. Her room was right underneath the attic.

Assuming that something, or someone, was bleeding on the top floor, the landlord dashed upstairs only to discover a completely deserted attic. There was no trace of a bleeding carcass, and the thick layer of dust on the floor suggested that no one had been in the room for quite some time. The old woman's suite was cleaned up, but the story of the bleeding ceiling quickly spread, and the landlord soon had to lock the room up due to a lack of tenants desperate enough to stay under the now infamous attic.

By the early 1980s, the years had taken their toll on Adam Griffon's old house on Constance Street. The once stately home had crumbled into an abandoned and dilapidated shell in one of New Orleans' less distinguished neighborhoods. While very few stories about Griffon House circulated during this time, among all the crumbling homes on the block, it was the only one that the city's destitute didn't use for shelter. It wasn't any harder to get into, but there were whispers about all the strange sights and sounds coming from the house. Occasional passersby claimed to see the faces of the two soldiers in the attic window. Others were said to hear the faint strains of song from within. And then there were those who only looked at the house and immediately sensed that there was something very wrong. A wrong, it seems, that no length of time will ever make right.

The Andrew Jackson Hotel

In the daytime, nothing about the Andrew Jackson Hotel suggests ghosts. With its pastel yellow walls, bright white window frames and freshly painted blue shutters, the hotel is one of the more cheerful buildings on Royal Street. Inside, the Andrew Jackson is free of ghostly stereotypes as well: no black cats slink through the shadows, no portraits with unsettling gazes follow guests across the room, the corners are free of cobwebs. Indeed, if there is any one building in the French Quarter that looks like it should be free of ghosts, the Andrew Jackson Hotel is the one. Yet if there is any truth to the stories that emerge from the Andrew Jackson, the spirits of the dead are hardly deterred by bright color schemes. According to local lore, the hotel is haunted by no less than five ghosts—juvenile, fun-loving ghosts, but ghosts nonetheless.

Local lore has it that a boys' school once stood where the hotel is today. That was before the two great fires of the late 1700s. The school was one of the many buildings reduced to ashes when the infernos ripped through the city. Thanks to the young pranksters that have remained behind, however, they were not quite forgotten.

Buildings were not all that was lost during the fires of 1788 and 1794. It is impossible to know exactly how many died during the blazes, but a good many of the French Quarter's ghost stories find their roots in the disasters, along with the restless souls who lost their lives and homes to the merciless conflagration.

The ghosts in the Andrew Jackson Hotel are said to be such spirits—the ghosts of five young boys who died when their

Voices of children playing in the courtyard can be heard in the middle of the night.

school was claimed by one of the fires. Next to nothing is known of these boys; their names are a mystery, as are their ages and the exact circumstances of their deaths. No one can even offer a visual description. But their voices are well known to those who have had close encounters with these ghosts from New Orleans' past.

They are invariably rambunctious, the sounds of their boisterous voices often loud enough to wake guests up from sleep. In the Andrew Jackson, it is common for guests to approach the front desk in the middle of the night, complaining of the children playing in the courtyard. Of course, at that time of night, there are no children playing in the courtyard. It does seem to be a favorite place for these five boys to congregate, though, and they seem to be especially fond of meeting there late at night, well after all the hotel's guests have gone to sleep. They aren't limited solely to the courtyard, however, and on occasion have been heard running through the halls, bickering in the lobby, and even once or twice hollering in the bedrooms.

As to what these boys are saying, their dialogue is said to be almost entirely limited to nonsense and child's play. There is laughter and shouting, puerile insults and equally fitting comebacks. The voices are French, and for the most part, they are all speaking at the same time, making it difficult to sort out individual speech from the tumult.

While they are certainly a nuisance to guests and employees at the hotel, at least it can be said that the boys are enjoying themselves. Whatever horrors they witnessed in 1794 have apparently been forgotten, and the early young Americans seems to be whiling away eternity with the same games they played while alive. Given the brutality of their demise, it could be much, much worse.

The Ghosts of Oak Alley Plantation

A gloomy winter day hangs over St. James Parish, and things are slow at the Oak Alley Plantation. The entire morning and early afternoon have passed without a single visitor to the historic site. Inside, a guide sits in the kitchen, using the quiet time to catch up on some reading. When she first hears the sound, it is so faint that she doesn't give it any thought. Certainly, it *sounds* like a horse-drawn carriage, but it is so distant that it could be anything. She doesn't even look up from the book. Yet within a few seconds, the sound has grown too loud to ignore. It is coming down the front road, she knows, and by the jingling of the harnesses, the clip-clop of hooves, the sound of wooden wheels rotating on their axles, she realizes it *is* a horse-drawn carriage. She puts her book down and walks to the door. By the time she gets there, the carriage sounds like it is right outside. She hears the driver shout as the horses are reigned in. She opens the door. A sudden chill shoots up her back at the sight that greets her. There is no one there. No driver, no carriage, no horses—just an empty lot under a dark gray sky.

A historical guide is taking a group through the plantation house. The guide and group come into a small room that has been modeled to look like a plantation overseer's office. The guide has begun her presentation, talking about the room and the tasks of the plantation overseer, when an unmistakable smell of cigar smoke suddenly rises in the room. The odor is so strong that the guide stops the presentation. The visitors smell it too, and they look around, perplexed.

No one has lit up a cigar, and there is no visible smoke in the air, but the smell is so strong that a few of the visitors have stepped out of the room. Unable to provide any explanation, the guide leads the visitors from the stifling room.

Another guide is leading visitors through the second floor of the plantation house where a chamber has been laid out as a replica of an antebellum sick room, complete with bed, religious symbols and medical supplies. The guide is just beginning to explain 19th-century medicine when she feels an ice-cold jolt up her back. In the next moment, she feels a heavy weight on her lungs, making it almost impossible to breathe. She does not panic, but quickly concludes her presentation of the makeshift infirmary and leads the group out. As soon as they step out of the room, the pressure eases off her lungs and she is able to breathe again.

Welcome to the Oak Alley Plantation. These are just some of the phenomena that are said to occur within the walls of the plantation house, a building that has become nearly as famous for its ghosts as it is for the two splendid rows of old oak trees that form its quarter mile "oak alley" to the banks of the Mississippi.

The trees were there first, planted in the early 1700s by some long-forgotten French settler. While the settler's identity will never be known, the grandeur of his thinking survives in the trees he planted nearly 300 years ago. With its two rows of 14 oaks that are planted 80 feet apart, the alley became a local landmark. As far back as the 1720s, the Capuchin priests who settled in the parish spoke of the oak alley. In the 1800s, river men on the Mississippi came to gauge their distance from New Orleans by the appearance of the lane of oak trees that led to the river's edge. A man-made lane that led to no man-made edifice, an impressive memento of some mysterious man's thwarted plans.

However, one man's thwarted plans proved to be the launching point for another's. Jacques Roman, one of the most powerful sugar planters in the South, purchased the land around Oak Alley in 1836. One year later, he began construction of the Classic Revival mansion that stands there today, right at the end of the oak tree-flanked lane. After more than a century, oak alley finally led to something.

With two and a half stories, the plantation was the heart of a 2400-acre sugar cane plantation that included a sawmill, overseer's houses, hospital and 24 slave cabins. By all accounts, Jacques Roman was an incredibly successful businessman, but he was nowhere near as fortunate with his domestic life. To say that his wife, Celina, was unhappy at Oak Alley is an understatement. A vivacious socialite, Celina lived for the good life, enjoying the revelry and opulence of the New Orleans elite. Jacques, on the other hand, was something of a hardworking recluse and preferred to live in the heart of his plantation, where his money was made. This difference led to no shortage of rows in the Oak Alley plantation, where Celina made sure that Jacques never got too comfortable tending to his business responsibilities, shouting out the case for living in New Orleans with tireless fervor.

Jacques was not so tireless, however, and he ended up dying of tuberculosis at the relatively young age of 48. Celina's ceaseless anger when Jacques was alive turned to ceaseless guilt after he passed on. It was said that she never recovered from her grief, wandering the plantation in a long black dress and veil, indifferent to all around her. She handed over the duties of running the plantation to the overseer, and

Oak Alley is as famous for its ghosts as it is for its two splendid rows of old oak trees.

she took many lavish trips downriver to New Orleans, but everyone could see that she had lost her enthusiasm for the things she used to love so much.

And yet it is quite possible that Celina wasn't grieving for husband alone. Tragedy seemed to take a particular liking to the Roman family. It befell Celina's daughter, Louise, in a freakishly gruesome accident. According to the legend, panic befell the plantation house when one of young Louise's gentlemen callers showed up on the doorstep in a state of extreme inebriation. Fully aware of how improper it would be for her daughter to receive a young man so intoxicated, Celina sent Louise upstairs to her room while she fended off the drunken lout. As Louise was running up the spiral staircase to the second floor, she tripped and fell. The steel boning in her big hoop skirt broke loose and punctured her leg.

It was a grisly wound that became immediately life-threatening when gangrene set in. There were no options besides amputation, and so it was that the wealthy planter's daughter, whose hand was once coveted by so many potential suitors, was deemed unmarriageable by the social standards of the time. After years of solitude in Oak Alley, Louise moved to New Orleans, though for a very different purpose than her mother. She founded a convent for Carmelite nuns in the Crescent City and lived the rest of her days there. She died of natural causes in her 80s, and her remains were entombed in the family crypt in New Orleans, along with her mother and father. Yet while their bodies are buried in New Orleans, some are convinced that their spirits made their way back to Oak Alley.

Like so many other southern plantations, Oak Alley fell into gradual disrepair after the Civil War. Following decades of abandonment and alternating owners, it was passed on to a non-profit organization in 1972. Designated a National Historic Landmark, it has become an attraction for history buffs who come from near and far to visit this fine example of antebellum southern architecture and, of course, the famous lane of oak trees. During these years, while the plantation house has been busy with tour guides, managers and visitors, all sorts of strange occurrences have been reported.

The overwhelming smell of cigar smoke in the overseer's room, the sounds of approaching carriages, the stifling pressure on the lungs in the second-floor sick room—these are just some of the phenomena that people are said to have witnessed. In her work, *Louisiana's Haunted Plantations*, Jill Pascoe relates the experiences of Oak Alley manager, Sandra Schexnayder:

> Having worked in the plantation for a number of years, Schexnayder was familiar with Oak Alley's ghost stories but had never actually witnessed anything herself. That changed one afternoon while she was sitting on a piano bench in the parlor, waiting for the last tour of the day to finish up. The tour group was on the second floor, and Schexnayder had locked all the doors herself, so she was more than a little surprised when she looked over and saw a woman standing near the staircase. Wondering how this woman could have gotten into the house, the manager stood up with the intention of approaching the mysterious woman. But she didn't have time to take a single step. The instant she was on her feet, the veiled woman turned around and vanished—blinking out of sight, just like that. It would be the first of many run-ins with the lady in black. Since then, she has spied the tail of a black dress swooshing around hallway corners, and has seen the lady appearing behind her, or drifting up the stairs to the second floor gallery.

Pascoe also writes of the experiences of Jane Landry, a tour guide who also had an encounter with the shrouded lady. One day in the winter of 2001, Landry found herself sitting alone in the Oak Alley kitchen, enjoying a cup of coffee and a moment of silence. Perfectly relaxed, she was suddenly hit by the feeling that she wasn't alone. Turning around, her blood froze at the sight of the woman in the long black dress, a veil over her face. The woman was standing no more than a yard and a half away, perfectly still and silent as she stared at the tour guide. Landry didn't bother asking any questions; she knew by the chills running up and down her back that the thing standing in front of her was not a living, breathing being. Only after a few seconds passed did she find the courage to move, swiveling around in her stool and running from the room in a panic.

According to Pascoe, both Schexnayder and Landry's descriptions of the lady in black were identical. Hardly a faded or transparent apparition, the woman appeared as solid and real as any living person. She appears "dressed all in black, with a black veil that comes halfway down her chest, hands clasped, and hair up."

Could it be the ghost of Celina Roman, still grieving the death of her husband? Or perhaps it is Louise Roman, finally able to walk in the afterlife, though still haunted by the loss of her limb? Both theories have been offered as possibilities, though she isn't the only spirit said to haunt Oak Alley.

The identity of the second ghost isn't too much of a mystery to anyone who sees him, for his portrait hangs in plain sight in the parlor. He is none other than the original plantation patriarch, Jacques Roman. Over the years, numerous people have spotted him dressed in anachronistic clothing, standing outside and staring in through the same window, looking decidedly unamused. Those who have seen him say he only appears for a second or two. The plantation owner then vanishes as quickly as he appeared, leaving bewildered witnesses with cold chills in their veins.

One more ghost has been spotted in Oak Alley, though there is no historical record of her identity. She has been described as a young auburn-haired girl wearing a white nightgown, no older than 12 years of age. Almost always appearing on the third-floor staircase, the girl has the same disturbing habit as the other two ghostly residents in the house—she vanishes into thin air after several seconds. While no one can say with any certainty who this girl is, according to Pascoe, visiting psychics claim that at one time, a 12-year-old died in the house, and that this is likely the sick girl's spirit.

And these are the ghosts that haunt Oak Alley Plantation. Or perhaps it should be said, the *visible* ghosts that haunt it. As chilling as the sightings of the lady in black, the girl in white and Jacques Roman may be to those who witness them, the sightings are not as common as the countless other phenomena that are said to occur throughout the house. Visitors and guides alike have experienced weird temperature deviations in all parts of the mansion; a spot in a hallway, room or staircase will suddenly get incredibly cold for a few seconds, then go back to normal. Lights have been known to flicker on and off by themselves; more than once, the rocking chair in the upstairs hallway has been seen rocking on its own; guides will often hear their names whispered to them when they are alone.

Could these, too, be the actions of the three ghosts that appear from time to time? Or are there other spirits in the house—perhaps several restless dead that cannot be seen but are just as active? As is usually the case with questions regarding the paranormal, no certain answer can be given. All that can be said for sure is that the tragedies of Oak Alley's past seem determined, in one way or another, to remain in the present.

Loyd Hall Plantation

The Fitzgerald family had farming, not historical preservation, in mind when they purchased the 640 acres of Loyd Hall Plantation in 1948. In fact, they did not even know the historical treasure was there. The long-neglected house was so overgrown that it was practically invisible when the buyers inspected the property by air. Only after the deed was signed did they discover that, in addition to the fertile farmland, they were also the owners of a bona fide antebellum plantation house.

Delighted, the Fitzgeralds decided they wanted to live in the old house, and little time was wasted before they began their restoration of the historic building. Today, the classic Georgian home is a monumental success story in home improvement, in which a little—or perhaps a lot—of elbow grease turned a neglected and overgrown wreck into a fine example of antebellum architecture in the South. Yet the visage of Loyd Hall's past was not all the Fitzgeralds brought back to life when they went about restoring their beloved new home.

There are ghosts in the plantation house—four ghosts, to be exact. As supernatural remnants of a tumultuous history, the spirits of Loyd Hall continue to tell their nearly forgotten stories in the attic, the creaky halls and the spacious chambers of the old house. The arrival of the Fitzgeralds brought an audience that would be able to witness this story. Because they were so pleased with the notion of residing in the plantation house, and because the spirits were easy to get along with, the Fitzgeralds lived alongside the phantoms of Loyd Hall's past. And when the family opened the plantation house to the public in 1989, the ghosts of Loyd Hall became more widely known.

It began in 1820, when an Englishman named William Loyd arrived in the region with bottomless pockets and ambitions to be a planter. He bought his 620 acres and built the classic plantation house, from which he oversaw his tobacco, sugarcane, cotton and indigo operation. There is the history book version of the people who lived in the Loyd plantation, and then there are the legends.

The history book version doesn't tell us much. William Loyd, the miscreant son of a wealthy British family, was essentially paid to get as far away from his kin as possible. After meeting his wife, Sarah, in Tennessee, this black sheep found his place in northern Louisiana, where he built the plantation house that stands there today. He died in 1864, leaving his wife and two sons behind, and they lived at the plantation until 1871. Almost nothing is known about the plantation house between 1871 until the Fitzgeralds purchased it in 1948, though it is said that the property changed hands 20 times.

The Loyd Hall legends are far more colorful. There is the sad tale of Inez Loyd, William Loyd's niece, a spurned woman who was almost wed in the plantation house. The legend tells us that her uncle had spared no expense: Loyd Hall was festooned in brilliant flowers and the best food and drink was provided for a houseful of illustrious guests. Inez herself was dressed in a wedding gown fit for royalty.

It was a cloudless summer day. The sun shone down on the brilliantly decorated house and the well-dressed congregation was abuzz with conversation. All they were waiting for was the groom, who was supposed to arrive at any time.

There may have been a few concerned whispers when, with an hour to go before the ceremony began, the groom had not yet shown up at Loyd Hall. Half an hour later, guests could see the anxious bride peeking out from behind the curtains of the third floor window, looking for the arrival of the man she had planned to marry. When the time for the ceremony's opening had come and gone, and the groom was still nowhere to be found, his absence was all anyone was talking about—that and poor, unfortunate Inez, who could be seen on the third floor, looming in her huge wedding gown, looking for some sign of her fiancé.

He never came. The minister and the congregation waited for another hour, and an hour after that, and still no sign. Inez was no longer hiding behind the curtains, but standing before the open window, in plain view of the congregation below, anguish written all over her face. Then, before a single guest could leave, she acted. Letting out a terrible shriek, the near-bride jumped through the window, plummeting to her death amid a shower of broken glass.

This wasn't the only account of tragic love that came out of the plantation house. During the chaos of the Civil War, another star-crossed pair played out their own dismal narrative on the plantation. Union troops had just occupied the area, and a group of them camped out in Loyd Hall. There was nothing odd about this; many plantation houses in the South became temporary barracks when Union soldiers passed through. But in Loyd Hall, one of the northern soldiers managed to fall in love with one of the ladies of the house.

In fact, the man had become so enamored that he decided to stay. Hiding himself in the attic when it was time for his company to press on, the Union soldier planned to wait a few days before emerging and declaring his intentions to marry. But he would never make it that long. Not one day had passed before the soldier was discovered by another woman in the house, who stumbled upon him as she was running errands in the attic. Startled in the darkness, the unknowing woman attacked the soldier, throwing a flurry of blind blows against the man. The fight became lethal when the woman felt her hands close around the barrel of a gun. A struggle for his weapon ensued and then was abruptly concluded with a single gunshot. The revolver had gone off in the pitch black of the attic, with the soldier at the wrong end of the barrel. A single bullet tore through his heart and he was dead in seconds.

It is impossible to know for certain what the woman who murdered the man felt, but it is likely she would not have felt too much remorse. He was wearing a Union uniform, after all, and for all the woman knew, she was acting in self-defense. So it was that the man was buried in the cellar, without grief or ceremony, just another dead blue coat in a war that claimed thousands.

This Union soldier wasn't the only man who lost his life on the plantation during the Civil War. The Loyd Hall patriarch, William Loyd, had never been content with a planter's life. He was good at it, certainly, but legend tells us that the man of the house had a side to his character that insisted upon more lively pursuits. Before the Civil War began, he spent much of his spare time antagonizing the neighboring Choctaw tribe—so much so that his house had once come under attack by the angry natives.

While Loyd was fortunate enough to emerge unscathed from his disagreements with the local natives, his itch for action would cost him his life during the Civil War. Not content to line up with the Confederate rank and file, Loyd decided to take on the highly dangerous work of espionage, and he spent several months as a double agent, working for both the Northern and Southern armies. His career as a spy was short, however. Soon found out by occupying Union forces, Loyd was promptly hanged from a tree on his plantation.

Of the four tragedies that mark Loyd Hall, the least is known of Sally Boston. She was one of the household slaves that took care of the Loyd children before the Civil War began. Almost nothing is known of Boston, only that she died suddenly and mysteriously. A picture of perfect health in the days before her demise, Sally was believed to be the victim of some foul plantation house plot. Word began to spread among the slaves that she had been poisoned. Who had done it? Theories abounded. Some said it was another slave who was jealous of Boston's favored position in the slave hierarchy. Others whispered that Boston suffered the vengeance of Mrs. Loyd, who suspected the nanny was having an affair with her husband. Of course, it could very well be that such theories were nothing more than speculation and distorted truths. Perhaps the Loyd Hall nanny simply died of natural causes. It is impossible to say. And yet her legend survives to this day, continuing to be borne out by the ghostly sightings believed to be the supernatural residue of her untimely end.

While the how and why of Boston's death may be a mystery, the strange goings-on in Loyd Hall have kept her memory alive. Soon after her death, residents of the house began talking about a black woman dressed in a crisp white dress moving quickly in witnesses' peripheral vision, disappearing the moment people turn to look. Almost always, these sightings were accompanied by a strong and sudden odor of cooking food, even when there was no one cooking in the kitchen. While this phenomenon was said to occur all over the house, it was most frequent in the back parlor, where the flashing glimpses of the black woman occurred with unnerving regularity. This wasn't all that occurred with unnerving regularity. There was also the matter of the candles, which had acquired the habit of flying off the mantle by themselves. More than one person claimed to see the woman slapping the candles off the mantle, then vanishing before anyone was able to confront her. Sally Boston? Perhaps. And if so, the fact that her spirit seems to favor the back parlor has prompted some to conclude that this was the room where she was poisoned.

Sally Boston is only one of the four restless spirits that continue to express their discontent. The ghost of Inez Loyd has also been spotted on numerous occasions. The succeeding Loyds who stayed on after William Loyd passed were haunted by a woman in a black dress drifting through the third-floor halls. Appearing before startled witnesses one moment, and vanishing the next, the woman was said to bear an exact resemblance to young Inez, save for her dress, which had changed from a bride's white to a mourner's black.

Apparently, Inez Loyd is still in the house—at least according to Beulah Davis, former housekeeper and current hostess of the historic hall. She is quoted by Jill Pascoe in *Louisiana's Haunted Plantations*: "I saw a tall, slender woman with long brown hair and a black dress. I was standing in that door at the end of the hallway, coming in from the back porch and I was looking into the kitchen doorway…She had a black dress on and was tall and slender…It was just like she disappeared into the woodwork. She just disappeared. One minute she was there and one minute she was gone."

Whatever the jilted bride is hoping to accomplish in the house, at least she isn't alone in her heartache. Over the years, footsteps have been heard coming from the house's top floor, pacing back and forth in a nervous cadence. People who have gone up to investigate have always found the attic abandoned.

There is also reason to believe this lovelorn spirit is able to tear himself away from the attic from time to time. On certain full moons, always at midnight, a man in Union uniform has been spotted on the upstairs balcony playing a violin, the strains of some sad tune drifting throughout the house and across the fields. And yet he isn't completely lost to grief. At one time, he was apparently able to devote attention to something besides his loss.

The second generation of Fitzgeralds that lived in the house included three young girls who spent quite a bit of time in the attic. It had been converted into a playroom for these youngsters, who soon began talking about their friend, "Harry." According to these girls, Harry was a young man with black hair dressed in a blue uniform with shiny brass buttons. He was always friendly to these girls, and though he was never spotted by any of the adults in the house, the girls never stopped talking about him. For his part, the long-dead Union soldier appeared to have grown attached to the Fitzgerald girls. In her account of the goings-on in Loyd Hall, Jill Pascoe narrates an incident in which one of the girls was bedridden after having one of her kidneys removed. According to Pascoe, this girl would later claim that "Harry" never left her side, watching over her from the foot of the bed every night, until she had convalesced completely. Of course, after the girls were grown and moved away, "Harry" went back to his pining ways, pacing the attic at all hours and playing his full moon laments on his violin on the balcony at midnight.

Yet of all these spirits, the most active is William Loyd, the adventure-loving scoundrel who founded the plantation on which he was executed. His spirit is said to be responsible for the almost daily phenomena that are experienced in the hall. The cold spots that mysteriously come and go in all parts of the plantation house are believed to be him. Loyd is also suspected of being the one with the wandering hands— ice cold hands that grasp exposed hands and touch unsuspecting visitors on their faces and the back of their necks. Not one of the alarmed individuals who have felt his touch has ever caught a glimpse of what touched them, though they almost always speak of an inexplicable sensation—a stern, commanding presence, felt but not seen, standing very, very near.

Apparently, the stern, commanding presence believed to be William Loyd keeps his ice-cold hands busy. Before the plantation house was opened to the public, when the Fitzgeralds still lived in it, there were countless cases of dinnerware being removed from a set table, only to reappear in some unlikely place days later. Napkins, forks, glasses, knives and spoons repeatedly went missing, turning up days later in bathtubs, under kitchen sinks, behind chesterfields, underneath beds.

While recent years have seen William Loyd relax such disruptive behavior, the mischievous spirit has stepped up his other activities. To this day, disembodied footfalls are heard all over the house, while invisible fingers often play simple tunes on the piano. Doors open and close by themselves, and the stereo has been known to turn itself off, replaced by crackling music from the hall's antique phonograph, which has been mysteriously turned on by the hand lever and cranked back to life.

These phenomena occur frequently enough that visitors to the Loyd Hall Plantation may very well experience a supernatural encounter. That said, anyone who has spent any time in the historic plantation will point out that while the spirits of Loyd Hall are certainly mischievous, none of them are malevolent in any way. While residents, staff and visitors have had all sorts of run-ins with the restless dead in this Louisiana plantation home, no one has ever felt threatened by them. These spirits seem to be content haunting for haunting's sake, and given the high level of ghostly activity here, there looks to be no end in sight.

2
Dark Legends of Louisiana

Voodoo in New Orleans

It began in Haiti, among slaves looking for meaning in the sweltering torture of the Caribbean plantations. They took what they were able to recall from the magic of their African homelands—the worship of ancestors, the belief in the gods they called the *loa*, the drums and the dances—and mixed them with the religion of their oppressors. Thus they recited the Lord's Prayer while dancing past exhaustion until possessed by spirit of Zombi. Thus they worshipped the Virgin Mary and in the same breath called upon the spirits of their deceased kin. They called it voodoo, and it was the folk religion of the oppressed—a dark and terrible force in the eyes of those who ruled over them.

Voodoo began to spread through Louisiana in 1791, when Haitian slaves began their bloody 13-year revolt against their French masters. Frightened plantation owners fleeing the island came to New Orleans, bringing their slaves with them, and with these slaves came the beliefs and rituals of their religion. Authorities in New Orleans initially reacted to this mysterious faith the same way the Haitian authorities had—they tried to smother it. They were unsuccessful.

The New Orleans voodoos' first meeting place was a brickyard on Dumaine Street. When police drove them away, they took to congregating in secret on the shores of Lake Pontchartrain or along the Bayou St. John. There they would meet after dark, the sound of their drums, their chants and their ecstatic shouts resounding through the swamp. The laws against voodoo were relaxed after 1803, when Louisiana became a territory of the United States.

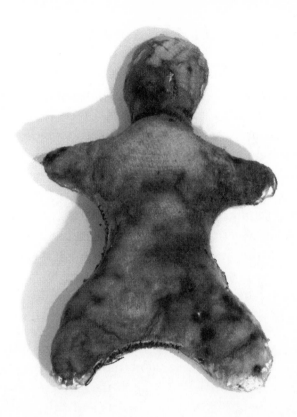

Dolls such as this one formed part of the voodoo culture in Louisiana.

In the 1800s, New Orleans saw voodoo's golden age. Priests and priestesses emerged from the French Quarter's woodwork, competing with one another for power over frightened followers. Voodoo-inspired dances were held publicly in Congo Square (Louis Armstrong Park today). Different forms of voodoo magic became well known. People learned to fear *mojo*, voodoo's black magic, and often sought audience with a priest or priestess for the blessing of *juju*, white magic. The most famous practitioners made money off *gris-gris*, small bags filled with everything from cayenne pepper to snakeskin and then enchanted by voodoo magic. *Gris-gris* were worn around the neck by people who paid for good fortune, or hidden within the possession of an enemy to bring bad luck.

Of all the priests and priestesses who claimed to possess voodoo magic, no one was as famous as Marie Laveau, renowned as the voodoo queen of New Orleans. She presided over the community of worshippers in the mid-19th century, her incredible influence over the city marking the high point of voodoo in America. Dreaded in her day, her legend continues to inspire inordinate fear. For though it's believed Marie Laveau passed away sometime in the 1800s, there is also reason to believe that her spirit lives on in the city that was once hers for the taking.

The Spirit of Marie Laveau

The tale is short on specifics. No one knows when the following events took place, or who, exactly, the individuals involved were, but it is known that the story began in a Bourbon Street bar, with three drunk men hollering at one another over the revelry of the French Quarter. They might have been locals, or they might have been among the out-of-town throng that flocked to the city for its live music, stiff drinks, spicy dishes and other attractions. They may have been old friends, or perhaps they'd met for the first time that night. No one knows.

What *is* known is that it was deep into a muggy Louisiana night, and the three drunks were talking back and forth about one of New Orleans' favorite topics: the dead. Specifically, they spoke about the city's legendary voodoo priestess, Marie Laveau, and whether or not there was any truth to the stories about her ghost haunting St. Louis Cemetery No. 1, where her famous tomb is located.

One of the men claimed to believe the stories; he brought up the fact that accounts of Marie Laveau's ghost had been around for so long, told and retold by so many people. It would be foolish, he said, to disregard the experiences of so many. Besides, he continued, lowering his voice, more than once he'd walked by the St. Louis Cemetery at night, every time aware of a vague unsettling feeling—a sense that something unnatural was lurking on the other side of the cemetery wall.

While the man sitting next to him didn't have much of an opinion on the matter of Marie Laveau's ghost, the third man was an adamant skeptic who also happened to be roaring drunk. It wasn't enough for this man to rebuke what the first man was saying; he felt it necessary to offer his objections *loudly*. So began the hollering match over the validity of an old New Orleans legend, which grew louder and louder with every drink.

It wasn't long before the argument escalated to a point at which the skeptic found that mere disagreement with the other man wasn't enough; it was time he *proved* there was no such thing as the ghost of Marie Laveau. The opportunity came when the neutral man, who'd been silent through much of the argument, presented a booze-addled resolution.

"Let's settle this with a wager," the inebriated man slurred. "If you're so sure that there's nothing to the stories of Laveau's ghost, I'll put down $30 that says you don't have the guts to go over the cemetery wall and…" He paused, trying to think of a suitable dare.

The man who believed in the ghost continued. "Drive an iron spike into Laveau's tomb," he said. "And I'll pay half the $30."

The skeptic didn't even pause to consider. "An iron spike into her tomb," he said. "No problem, gentlemen."

The three men finished their drinks and stepped out onto Bourbon Street. They left the crowded, noisy thoroughfare behind, walking the Vieux Carre's darkened streets towards North Rampart Street, and across to the walls of St. Louis Cemetery No. 1. The skeptic carried an iron spike and a hammer they'd procured somewhere along the way. The man looked from the faces of the two other men to the cemetery wall, drab and cracked, faintly illuminated by the crescent moon. Away from the revelry of the French Quarter, now close by the city's oldest cemetery, the mood between the men had grown somber.

The skeptic stood there for a long moment, looking uncertain about what he was about to undertake. The neutral man spoke up. "You sure you want to do this?"

The man threw his shoulders back at the question. There would be no backing down. "I said I'd do it. I'll do it," he said. He tucked the hammer and spike into the inside pocket of the long coat he was wearing. "Now help me over this wall."

The men crouched low and clasped their hands together, forming a step for the skeptic, who flashed a single grin and then vaulted over the wall to the rows of tombs on the other side. The pair heard him land. "You okay?" one of them asked.

There was a moment of silence before a response came. "Fine," the man's voice came, tense, a few octaves higher than it had been before. It was obvious to the pair that he was spooked. Thinking of the row of sepulchers he must be looking at on the other side of the wall, neither of them blamed him. "Alright," the skeptic spoke again. "I'm off to find Laveau's tomb. I'll be back soon. Don't you be going anywhere."

"Course not," one of the other men said. They heard the skeptic's footfalls as he ran into the cemetery.

The two men stood and waited. Five minutes passed— then 10. After the first half hour, one of them pulled out a flask, took a swig and passed it on. The silence grew heavy, the darkness pervasive. They tried to kill their growing foreboding with wisecracks. Passing the flask back and forth, they made a few quips about what was taking the man so long. But the jokes were half-hearted, and their laughter sounded small and desperate in the looming darkness. Humor began to dissolve into desperation after the first hour.

Two hours later he still hadn't returned. The men, angry now, were shouting over the wall, calling for the missing man. Yet for all their insults and exhortations, they received nothing but silence in return. Not a sound came from the other side.

And that's the way it was for the rest of the night. The pair had long given up their shouting when the sun came up. It's impossible to say what they were thinking when the cemetery gates opened that morning and they rushed between the rows of tombs, straight for the place of burial of Marie Laveau. What were they expecting to see? Perhaps the stake and hammer at the foot of the tomb and a note thanking them for the $30? Or maybe the man still there, stone drunk, passed out? Could either of them dreamed up the sight that was waiting for them at Marie Laveau's tomb? Likely not.

The skeptic lay sprawled against the tomb of New Orleans' legendary voodoo priestess, one side of his trench coat pinned by the iron spike driven into the sepulcher wall. He was dead. It was obvious by one glimpse at his face, which was as pale as bone and stretched into an expression of wide-eyed terror. One cold hand still clutched the hammer. He'd gone ahead and driven the spike into the tomb after all, though it ended up costing him his life.

There was no visible wound. It was discovered later that he died of massive coronary arrest, perhaps having seen something so terrifying it shut his heart down. The most popular theory suggests that the booze-addled man accidentally pinned his coat to the tomb while hammering in the stake. He may have tried running from something that came out of the dark, but could only make it as far as the length of his coat. Thus the man found himself face-to-face with something so terrifying that the sight of it caused his heart to burst, and he fell dead.

The real question is, what appeared before the man when he was pinned to the tomb? What filled him with such fear that it caused his heart to stop? According to some, this is no real question at all. He'd come face-to-face with the voodoo queen herself—the ghost of Marie Laveau, who, needless to say, wasn't too pleased at having her resting place vandalized. Certainly, she wasn't one to be trifled with while she was alive.

New Orleans' most famous voodoo priestess, Marie Laveau, rose from undistinguished origins to become *the* matriarch of the Vieux Carre. While it is agreed that she was born sometime in the 1790s, biographies differ on her place of birth, some claiming that she was an immigrant from one of the Caribbean islands, others that she was born in the French Quarter. Either way, it is known that she was free black woman, probably the daughter of a plantation owner and his slave mistress, and that she would grow to become one of the most feared and respected citizens in the city, the "Bosswoman of New Orleans."

Laveau didn't acquire her status from any formal social institution. She was a black woman living in the Old South; no school, no church, no profession and no political body existed that would allow her an opportunity for any real power. Laveau's authority came from someplace else—from the fear and darkness that loomed on the fringes of respectable society, from the power of a religion that few at the time had the courage to refute. She was New Orleans' voodoo

The tomb of Marie Laveau has hundreds of visitors each year, and many have etched Xs into her sepulcher in hope that she still grants wishes.

queen, and it was her station as high priestess of a cult few people understood that granted her undeniable sway over the city on the swamp.

The Vieux Carre was Marie Laveau's stage, and she strode though it with purpose. Taller than most men of her day, she often wore long dresses of blue cotton and big gold hoops in her ears, and she tied her hair high with bright cloth. Her features were regal and haughty, and she rarely smiled in public. She was a woman who well understood the power of appearances and definitely took pains to maintain hers.

Yet she didn't rely on appearances alone. Of all the self-proclaimed voodoo practitioners in New Orleans, no one was as effective as Laveau. She was famous for an uncanny clairvoyance, able to divine all sorts of personal details about people she'd just met. And unlike so many of her peers, Laveau's voodoo magic was disturbingly effective. While there would've been a good number of voodoo priestesses in her day offering their magical services for a price, everyone knew that not a single priestess in town could compete with Laveau's gris-gris.

Not that her magical services came cheap. In the 1830s, a local patriarch went to her for help with his son, who was in court facing a rape charge. The evidence was stacked heavily against the defendant, and it seemed certain that he was going to be found guilty. The father of the accused was a wealthy man, and he promised Laveau a house on Rue Ste. Anne if she was able to have his son acquitted.

The young voodoo priestess agreed to help, assuring the man his son would be a free man the following day. That night she went to the St. Louis Cathedral to pray with three guinea peppers under her tongue. While three guinea peppers and a prayer hardly qualify for a legal defense, they did wonders for the offender in this case. Marie showed up in court and had the three peppers secretly placed under the judge's chair. That same day, the judge decided there was insufficient evidence against the accused, and the young man was dismissed of all charges. Soon after that, Marie Laveau moved into her new house on Rue Ste. Anne.

Was there a spell on the peppers—some mysterious voodoo mojo that allowed Marie to control the judge? Perhaps, though some have been quick to come up with alternate theories. Marie Laveau might not have relied entirely on voodoo magic to secure her influence. She was also the center of an information network that stretched throughout the entire city. In practically every prominent New Orleans household, there were servants who answered to the voodoo queen, reporting everything that went on in the homes of the city's most powerful families. Some people have theorized that Laveau probably owed more of her supposed clairvoyance to these spies rather than any proclaimed talent with voodoo magic. According to skeptics, the three peppers weren't enchanted, but were more likely a message for the judge, a reminder of some secret Laveau held over him. Whatever the case, whether it was voodoo magic or simple blackmail, there was no denying the outcome: Marie Laveau, a black Louisianan woman in the 1830s, had intimidated a judge into doing as she wished. And she got paid for it. Money, it seems, was Laveau's greatest motivator, and voodoo magic wasn't her only business. Indeed, her other operations—she was a hairdresser and also ran a brothel on the edge of town—only provided her with even more potential blackmail information.

Even if Laveau's real power came from household spies, beauty salon gossip and an incriminating list of johns, she was still an expert at dressing it up in the trappings of voodoo. There wasn't a priestess in New Orleans who could compete with Laveau when it came to voodoo ritual. Involving enormous serpents, heavy rum consumption, animal sacrifice and feverish music and dance, the dramatic ceremonies formed the heart of the voodoo faith. A certain stage presence was required of the priestesses who presided over them, and it's said no one could hypnotize a crowd like Marie Laveau.

She often danced entwined within a serpent, Le Grand Zombi, and her rhythmic movements, fluid and unsettling, transfixed followers and spectators alike. She would sit on her throne, directing the faithful men and women who participated in her rituals, and the dances often went on for hours. Frenzied participants jumped, twitched and writhed to the manic beats until rum and exhaustion sent them into trance-like states. It was believed that at this point they were possessed, taken over by the *loas*, the supernatural entities worshipped by the faithful.

It's up the reader to decide whether Laveau had a genuine connection with voodoo spirits, or whether she was merely an expert at manipulating crowds. Either way, she presided over the most impressive ceremonies of her time. Hundreds of people attended her yearly St. John's Eve rituals, which began on the evening of June 23 and continued all night until the sun rose the following morning. With massive bonfires, animal sacrifice, nude dancing and simulated orgies, the St. John's ceremonies were always spectacular, drawing the largest crowds. Laveau, forever the entrepreneur, charged accordingly. And as her purse swelled, so too did her fame.

Many of the spectators were reporters looking for a story, and Laveau's mystique grew as news of her ceremonies spread. In the end, she was more a legend than a living, breathing person. As she grew old, Marie Laveau stopped appearing on the streets of the Vieux Carre, and sent her daughter, Marie II, in her stead. The younger Laveau bore a remarkable resemblance to her mother, and she went about her business as though she actually was. By that time, few would've dared to question her identity, and it was gradually accepted by many New Orleans residents that somehow the voodoo queen's youth had been unnaturally extended. In actuality, the first Laveau passed away in 1881, an emaciated old woman who'd long since lost her wits. Marie II died 16 years later, in 1897.

But their story does not end there. Between the two of them, the name Marie Laveau ruled over voodoo in New Orleans for almost a century; it would not be easily forgotten in a city so obsessed with its dead. People weren't about to leave Marie Laveau alone just because she had passed away. What was death to a voodoo queen? She was able to aid people while she lived; surely she would be able to do the same from the grave. Thus, of all New Orleans' historic kirkyards, Laveau's purported resting place in St. Louis Cemetery No. 1 became the city's most visited tomb. Believers came from near and far with hopes that the deceased priestess would grant them their wishes.

Evidence of these requests is written plainly on Laveau's tomb. It became custom for supplicants to etch a row of three Xs into the sepulcher for their wishes, and it wasn't long before the tomb was covered in row upon row of these crude markings. To this day, the rows of Xs are plainly visible, a chaotic scrawl of tipped crosses over crumbling white plaster. Some might be surprised to see that many of these Xs have obviously been carved quite recently. In addition, the tomb is always cluttered with gifts of pennies, flowers and beaded necklaces. It's obvious to any visitor that there are those who still believe in the power of the long-deceased voodoo queen.

Long deceased, indeed, but according to legend, hardly restful. The stories about the goings-on after nightfall in St. Louis Cemetery No. 1 have been around for years now. Early testimonials described a lone black woman, tall and regal, in a flowing dress and a high turban, walking among the tombs of the cemetery by the light of the moon. Always spotted near her tomb, she would remain visible for no longer than a few moments before vanishing suddenly—there one instant, gone the next.

The appearance of the apparition wasn't the only evidence that Marie Laveau's spirit wasn't ready to depart. Far more incredible were the spectral St. John's Eve rituals said to take place around Laveau's tomb. It's impossible to say who witnessed the first one, or when, but the tale has been repeated enough to earn its place in the annals of New Orleans legend.

One of the better-known sightings involves a young man in the 1930s. According to the story, the young man was unemployed, forced to vagrancy by the hard conditions of the Great Depression. Without a job or a home, he had taken to sleeping in St. Louis Cemetery No. 1 throughout much of June. The night of the 23rd would be the last time he did so. Just like he had on previous nights, the man clambered atop one of the tombs to sleep on the roof.

Sometime in the night, he was jolted awake by heavy drums and human voices chanting somewhere in the darkness. The noise—rhythmic, steady, yet infused with a frightening zeal—was like nothing he had ever heard before. The sounds were unfamiliar, but the man found he had no desire to acquaint himself with the people who were making them. The desperate voices and driving drums sent chills up his neck, and he knew in his bones that that he wasn't meant to hear whatever was transpiring. As quietly as he could, the man climbed down from the top of the tomb and crept through the cemetery, looking for the nearest exit.

What he found instead, as he rounded a corner between the rows of sepulchers, was the most terrifying spectacle he would ever lay his eyes upon. There, in a circle surrounding one of the tombs, was a large group of vaguely transparent men and women, half-clothed, enshrouded in glowing red mist, chanting in time to the beat of invisible drums. They danced as they chanted, their movements lewd and uninhibited to the horrified man's eyes. In the middle of this, next to a tomb covered in Xs, stood a woman who was easily six feet tall. She stood imperious, enmeshed within an enormous serpent and surveying the dancers with eyes that burned with devilish intensity. The man knew at once that everything before him—the drumming, the chants, the dancers— was there because of her. She was causing it all. Without wasting a single second, he turned and ran, dashing pell-mell through St. Louis No. 1 and vaulting over the wall, never to return.

No one can say for certain if this man was the first person to witness the ghostly voodoo ceremony on St. John's Eve, but he certainly wasn't the last. Throughout the years, strange phenomena have been reported in the old New Orleans cemetery after sunset on June 23. Some claim to have heard faint chanting and the sounds of drums while walking by the cemetery walls. Others with more adventurous inclinations have ventured into the cemetery to see firsthand the spectacle of the supernatural ceremony taking place around Laveau's tomb.

While the red-tinged apparitions haven't appeared consistently every June, the ceremony has been spotted enough times to keep the legend of Laveau alive. To this day, people continue to request favors of the voodoo queen. Countless supplicants still scratch their Xs into her tomb and leave offerings of flowers and pennies, perhaps hoping that she is just as capable of granting wishes dead as she was while living. Whatever the case, there's one thing for certain; if there's any truth to the St. John's Eve sightings, she still knows how to throw the best voodoo soirée in town.

The Ghost of the Raccourci Cut-Off

Among the boatmen of the Mississippi, a man's skill at navigating the broad, black waters was always something to brag about. Many nights, in the countless taverns that dotted its riverbanks, drunken men shouted their bravado, claiming that there was no other man in that town, in that parish, in the entire state, who knew the Mississippi better. Someone would boast that he and his boat were unsinkable, that the river's course was etched into the lines on his palm. Another would boast louder that he had spent so many years on the mighty river that its muddy waters ran through his veins. When this man cast off into the Mississippi's currents, he wasn't just navigating the river; he *was* the river. And so on.

Well, one dark night, in one such tavern, the beer and braggadocio were flying thicker than usual. The tavern was packed full of boatmen—men who would normally be out on their runs, but who dared not on this evening—dared not because something strange seemed to have happened to the Mississippi after the sun had gone done down, because the heaviest fog any of them had ever seen was hanging over the river, because the river itself seemed restless, angry—churning in bizarre eddies, pulling this way and that in unusual currents. One man in the tavern had whispered that the devil was in the Mississippi that night, and nothing, living nor dead, belonged upon its back.

But as is usually the case with boastful men, the greater the fear, the louder the boast, and the empty conceit among the boatmen was especially vocal in the tavern, growing with every beer thrown back. Their proclamations of courage grew ever more outrageous as the fog grew thicker, creeping into the bar in slow, billowing tendrils, which the men were doing their best to ignore. And then, one young man decided he had had enough.

"Enough of this!" he cried out, and the boldness in his voice silenced everyone. Here, they instantly recognized, was someone willing to confront the fear of the river. "I've gotten more'n my fill of all you, yellow blowhards. You're all too scared to be out on that river tonight, and what's more you all know it! Well not me. I'll show you what a real boatman looks like. I'm heading out there right now to finish my run!"

The men in the bar laughed. One shouted back that the fog was too thick, that he wouldn't be able to see a thing ahead of him, and he would run aground on one of the banks before he made it 100 yards. Another voice called out that the fog would frighten him and he would be back before midnight.

"Say what you will," the young man replied, "but I swear right here that once I'm on the water, I won't be turn back for nothing—even if Lucifer himself is out there on the river."

And with these words, he departed, getting on his paddle-boat and turning his back forever on the tavern, the river-bank and the land of the living. For an hour or so, he thought he was going to make it. With his boat bell ringing and his lantern lit, he made his way along the river. True, the current was erratic and unusually strong; more than once, he almost ran his boat aground in the freakishly strong eddy. But the boatman was sure of himself. He'd made the run countless times before and could navigate the river with his eyes closed—or so he thought.

Was the devil truly in the river that night?

He was near the Raccourci cut-off when he saw the river-bank emerge out of the fog in front of him. The boatman was stunned. It was impossible. There was no bend in this branch of the river. He was sure of it. It should have been straight-ahead. He made a sharp turn and thought he was back on track, when again the riverbank appeared in front of him. Impossible. Was the Mississippi shifting before his very eyes? Was the devil truly in the river that night?

The boatman began to curse loudly, his long and continuous string of expletives ringing against the shoreline. Recalling his vow at the tavern, he knew that he didn't have a choice; he would have to continue ahead. No matter what, he couldn't turn back and face the jeering men in the tavern. And he wouldn't have to, ever again.

At that moment, his boat jarred violently as his engine died. We will never know what was going through the young man's mind when the boat jolted again and then turned over into the black current. The boat sank to the bottom of the Mississippi, taking its captain with it.

But according to some, this wasn't the end of the brave boatman's journey down the Mississippi. For on certain nights, it is said you can hear his bell and his curses as he desperately pilots his way down the river. Though no boat is visible on the river, there's a lone ball of light, the glow of his lantern, which remains visible for a few minutes before vanishing into the darkness at the precise moment the bells and the curses fall silent. It is a ghostly memento of the night the devil was in the Mississippi River, and of the brash young man who thought he could defy it.

The Sultan's Palace

It looms on the corner of Dauphine Street and Orleans Avenue. The Gardette-Le Pretre House, an enormous four-story apartment that, when it was constructed in 1836, stood as one of the tallest buildings in the Vieux Carre. Throughout the first half of the 1800s, it was a regal dwelling, owned by a prominent Creole banker named Jean Baptiste Le Pretre, one of the city's moneyed elite. Le Pretre's home was known for its opulence; with its expansive top-floor ballroom, lush velvet curtains, glittering chandeliers, polished floors and impressive cast-iron galleries, the mansion was designed with extravagant entertainment in mind. The lodging fit the occupant perfectly. Le Pretre himself was a known *bon vivant*, and for many years, the house was put to good use. People grew used to hearing the sounds of music and laughter on the Dauphine and Orleans intersection, and locals came to equate the big building with sumptuous revelry.

And yet, it seems as if Le Pretre was a bit *too* enamored with the good life. Sometime after the 1850s, the banker ran into serious financial difficulties. Deeply in debt, with a lifestyle that saw him sinking further into insolvency every the month, Le Pretre was on the brink of ruin. He was forced to put his beloved mansion up for rent. And so begins one of New Orleans' darkest legends.

Unless Le Pretre was a fan of *The Arabian Nights,* it's likely that in his wildest dreams, he wouldn't have been able to imagine his future tenant. It's said "the Turk" weighed anchor in New Orleans late one evening, his ship near bursting with a fortune in gold and jewels, a small army of eunuch bodyguards and a huge harem of women and young boys.

The man's identity was a mystery to the citizens of the city, but rumors quickly began to spread. Some theorized that he was a deposed Sultan of some distant Middle Eastern kingdom. He definitely fit the part, with his bright silks, towering turban and cadre of saber-wielding guards. Whoever he was, and whatever had brought him to New Orleans, it quickly became clear that he and his entire retinue was intent on settling there.

The sultan's timing was perfect. Le Pretre had just begun looking for a tenant, and his mansion was one of the only available buildings in town with room enough for the sultan's court. A deal was struck, and the Turk's servants began unloading the ship. It would have been difficult to be inconspicuous about it. With a shipload of riches, brilliant silks and bizarre furniture, to say nothing of the harem and the personal army, the move from the dockyards to the Vieux Carre attracted all sorts of attention. By the time the sultan had settled in to his new home, he was the talk of the town—whether he wanted to be or not.

The sultan may have been trying to keep a low profile. He was almost never seen outside his home, and he made it clear from the onset that visitors were not welcome. The doors to the main courtyard were always locked and barred, and people who stood and stared at the windows for too long always found themselves face-to-face with one of the Turk's scowling guards. Not a single townsperson was ever invited into the "sultan's palace."

Yet despite—or perhaps because of—all his attempts at maintaining privacy, talk of the sultan seemed to increase with each passing week. While the intense security he kept up around his house did work in keeping people out, it also succeeded in piquing an already fascinated people's interest. The fact that the doors were barred and heavily guarded only made people more conscious of the fact that inside was a harem and an incredibly wealthy man from some incredibly alien place. And then there were the sounds that came out of the house. Shouts, laughter and strange music were heard at all hours. Some claimed to spy dancing silhouettes in the upper windows. Every day, there seemed to be another delivery of some foreign-looking item—whether a strange piece of furniture, exotic animal or collection of bizarre curios.

Rumors spread about the sorts of things that were going on behind the closed doors of the "sultan's palace." There was always someone who claimed to know someone who had succeeded in sneaking in and witnessed, firsthand, all sorts of unspeakable depravities. According to these stories, there were unbridled orgies in which the sultan sated his lusts on women and young boys alike. People said a cloud of opium smoke hung permanently over all the rooms, and no one did anything except sit idle in a drugged stupor all day. It was a picture of debauched hedonism that was extreme even by New Orleans standards. But it wouldn't last.

All it took was one night. A few of the sultan's neighbors might have wondered if anything was wrong when an entire evening passed without a sound coming from within the mansion. There were no strange musical instruments to be heard, no laughing or screaming. All night long, not a single guard was seen patrolling the front door. No lights shone from the windows, and there was no trace of movement. There was nothing but dead silence.

Curiosity quickly became alarm, however, when a woman walking down Dauphine Street early the next morning noticed something on the street that made her start. It was blood, a lot of blood—a long red stream was flowing out from under the front entrance of the sultan's palace. The woman shouted her discovery, and a crowd a soon started to form around the mansion. The authorities arrived not long after that and, when their calls into the house went unanswered, they battered down the front door.

The sight that greeted the first officers when they entered was instantly burned into the pages of New Orleans legend. As the spectators crowded outside craned their necks to catch a glimpse of what was inside, more than one of the police officers inside were on the verge of running out in sheer revulsion. The sultan's palace had been turned into a slaughterhouse. Everyone inside, every last retainer and concubine, had been murdered.

And not just murdered, but mutilated. The mansion was a gore-splattered mess, with body parts and viscera littered in each and every room, from the basement to the top floor. The macabre chaos of bloody body parts was so bad that it was impossible to know which limbs had belonged to which body. No gunshots had been fired the night before. The victims had met their end silently, on sharp steel.

As for the sultan himself, his fate was no better than those of his servants. His maimed body was found in the garden, half buried underneath an olive tree. One arm was clawing at dirt, the other arm was buried along with the rest of his body. His tortured face, covered with soil, poked out just above the surface. It was evident that he had choked to death on the dirt, leading investigators to conclude that his killers had cut him badly and then buried him alive. According to the legend, his dead body lay under a date tree, in which a marble tablet hung. Arabic script was carved into the tablet, reading: "The justice of heaven is satisfied, and the date tree shall grow on the traitor's tomb."

What had the sultan done to justify such brutal actions? Who had he betrayed? These were just another two unanswerable questions in a mysterious legend full of question marks. All the theories that have come up are nothing more than creative speculation. There were stories about a vengeful brother who, enraged at the sultan for stealing his wife and his fortune, chased him around the world to exact his revenge. Some claimed that on the night of the massacre, a ship that looked much like the sultan's silently anchored on the docks and then left again later on that morning, before sunrise. Could the assassins have been on this ship? Perhaps, if anyone had actually *seen* it. The truth of the matter is that no such ship was spotted or reported by anyone on the docks. Like practically everything else about the sultan and his brutal demise, the story is nothing more than hopeful conjecture.

Things in the Gardette-Le Pretre house changed dramatically after the massacre. If it's true, as so many paranormal enthusiasts maintain, that ghosts are psychic impressions of traumatic circumstances they suffered prior to their deaths, then it's clear why the mansion on Orleans Avenue is crawling with so many restless spirits. Though no one occupied the mansions for years after, the stories about strange goings-on within its walls began to circulate almost as soon the house was cleaned out.

The sultan's activities in the mansion, in life as well as in death, remain unsolved.

The community still hadn't come to grips with the massacre when the first chilling sounds were heard at night from within the house. Sometimes it was music, laughter and revelry; other nights, it was screams and moans of people running through the halls and doors being slammed. Everyone knew that the mansion was empty, but it wasn't uncommon to spot figures in the windows: women with covered faces staring down at the street below just after sunset, a silhouette of a man with a turban, shadows moving quickly across the glass.

In the late 1800s, the mansion was converted into apartments to house the influx of Italian immigrants to the city. By all accounts, many of the new residents were tormented by the specters in the house. They were chased around by visions of dismembered guards, kept awake by the sounds of Middle Eastern flutes, shouts, laughs and sometimes terrible screams. More than one person claimed to have been woken by the sultan himself. He usually appeared at the foot of an eyewitness' bed, wearing his turban and silks, staring blankly at the horrified tenant for a few moments before slowly turning and vanishing into the darkness.

The latest reports of weird phenomena in the Gardette-Le Pretre house are found in the frequently cited *Times-Picayune* article, "Sultan's House, Life with an 'Exotic Ghost,'" which was printed in 1979. The article reports the testimony of two women, Virgie Posten and Jean Damico. Posten, who had lived on the ground floor in the late 1950s, claims to have frequently spotted a man in outlandish eastern dress. According to Posten, there was no pattern to the appearances. The apparition did not favor a particular room or time of day to manifest himself, but was just as likely to appear in the bathroom in the morning as in the kitchen during the afternoon. While the spirit never failed to startle her, Posten never felt threatened by the vision and learned to live with her ghostly roommate. One night, in one single terrifying instant, all that changed.

Posten was in her sitting room with a friend when their conversation was interrupted by the sound of footsteps in the hall outside her door. The steps were heavy and brisk, pacing back and forth right outside her suite. Posten opened her door and looked down the hall, but there was no one there. She'd been living with the sultan's ghost for some time now, and so was able to close the door with a shrug. *Just the sultan up to his tomfoolery again*, she thought. Sitting back down, she and her friend had just picked up where they had left off when they were interrupted again—this time by something far more difficult to ignore.

The shriek that sounded from the hall made the glasses rattle on the table. Posten and her friend started in fear, instinctively covering their ears. Both of them knew by the instant chill in their bones that the ear-splitting cry was not human. There was no way the sound from the other side of the door could have been produced by natural means. They didn't just register it through their ears; they heard it through their eyes, the pores of their skin, down their spinal columns. Both of them ran out of the apartment. Virgie Posten would never return to her home.

The other incident covered in the *Times-Picayune* article takes place roughly 10 years later. Jean Damico and her husband had bought the house in 1966 with plans to renovate and rent out its suites. She grew wise to the legends soon after purchasing it, when her neighbors warned her of all the freakish occurrences. Yet Damico, a skeptic when it came to such things, didn't give the stories too much thought.

Then came the late-night visit.

She was in her bed trying to get to sleep when she saw him in the darkness—a figure, a man, standing at the foot of her bed, looking at her. A frisson of panic seized her, and she lay frozen in horror, unable even to say a word. Seconds went by, each one a lifetime for Damico, who lay there still, immobilized by fear. And then, the figure moved, taking a step toward the bed. That was all Damico needed. Instantly jolted out of her paralysis, she lunged for the lamp on her night table. Fumbling with the switch, she only turned away from the approaching figure for an instant. She turned back to the man the moment she was able to flick the light on, but there was nobody there. The figure she saw had vanished along with the dark. That night Damico slept with the lights on.

After the incident, Jean Damico suddenly got interested in the Gardette-Le Pretre's past. While learning her new home's brutal history, she was especially drawn to the part about the sultan being partly buried under a tree in the courtyard. She knew now why the bare and twisted tree in the courtyard always seemed so unsettling.

And yet, unlike Virgie Posten, Jean Damico stayed on in the building. Has she come to some kind of understanding with the ghosts that are said to haunt the former sultan's palace? Or have the spirits finally gotten fed up with lingering over their gruesome deaths, and moved on? It's impossible to say, though one thing is certain: after talking to the people at the *Times-Picayune*, Damico has been quite reluctant to come forward about the occurrences in her home. Indeed, ever since the 1979 article, there have been no other accounts of weird occurrences within the old building. Maybe the sultan and his entourage have finally found their long-overdue peace. At last, some might say, though it might be prudent not to speak too soon. Because if nothing else, the sultan was mysterious, and for all anyone knows, he's waiting for just the right wind on just the right night to carry his vessel back to town.

Le Mythe du Loup-Garou

Everyone knows what werewolves are. The mythic creatures—human just like everyone else in daylight, raging wolf-beasts by the light of the moon—have been present in folk legend for millennia. As far back as Herodotus, writing in the 5th century B.C., there were stories of people who were able to change themselves into wolves. The great Roman poet Ovid penned the poem about brutal King Lycaon, who was cursed with a beastly wolf-form by angry gods. Time and again, in different cultures all around the world, the werewolf has appeared in one form or another: from the myths of ancient Greece to terror-stricken whispers in medieval villages, to the spiritual narratives of Native American legend. But of all cultures, none have shown such a fascination with the werewolf as the French.

This cultural preoccupation finds its roots in the Middle Ages, when the French seemed to have inordinate problems with vicious monsters, the *loups-garous*, that were said to terrorize villages across the countryside. In some places, the problem was perceived as being so bad that the authorities had to get involved. The government of the city of Dole passed an ordinance in 1572 encouraging local hunters to track down and kill the creatures. Throughout the 1600s, hundreds of people all over the country were tried and convicted as werewolves and put to death. The infamous wolves of Gevaudan were said to have killed over 60 villagers in the 1760s.

And when the French came to the New World, they brought their peculiar fascination with the *loup-garou* with them. Wherever they settled in North America, stories of

By the light of the moon, the loups-garous gather in the cypress trees on the edge of the bayou.

werewolves stalking the darkness on the edge of town followed. Parents used tales of the *loup-garou* to keep children indoors at night. And for those inclined to shirk their religious duties, the legend of the *loup-garou* kept them going to church. Being bitten by a werewolf wasn't the only way a person might sprout excessive body hair and become prone to howling at the moon; it was also said that someone who missed too many Sunday masses might develop homicidal nocturnal habits.

So it was that stories of the *loup-garou* made their way through Canada and the United States. In Quebec, there were tales of packs of werewolves doing the devil's bidding in flying canoes. In Vincennes, Indiana, the exorbitant number of werewolf legends can be traced back to the French fur traders who settled on the Wabash River in the early 18th century. And in Louisiana, the arrival of the French exiled from Acadia brought the *loup-garou* to the South. While there are stories of these French werewolves all over the state, the definite center of *loup-garou* activity is in the swampland around Bayou Goula, in Iberville Parish.

It is here that the creatures are said to gather every St. John's Eve for the ball of the *loups-garous*. From all over the parishes they come, guided by some mysterious force, to gather in the cypress trees on the edge of the bayou. Dozens of lupine beasts with glowing eyes, coarse hair and sharp canines come together in the sultry darkness, filling the night with a chorus of barks, snarls and deep rumbling growls. Then, all at once, as if prompted by some unseen signal, the creatures raise their snouts to the sky and send up a cacophony of long, high-pitched howls. The disturbing chorus continues, and a vague rhythm forms from the chaos. This is when the ball begins. One by one, the *loups-garous* fall in line, one behind the other, forming an enormous circle. They then stand on their hind legs and begin to walk in a circle, all the while sustaining their weird chorus as they go. It's the ball of the *loup-garou*, and it continues for hours until, without cause or warning, it suddenly stops. The creatures cease their howling and fall back upon all fours. Loping off in separate directions, they disperse as quickly as they came, vanishing into the black swamp with hardly a sound.

Where do these *loups-garous* come from? Who are they during daylight hours? While it's impossible to know their identities while in wolf form, according to the many tales, each of them are unique in how they spend their evenings.

There are, of course, the stories of communities being terrorized by these beasts—farmers waking to find some of their cattle slaughtered, larders sacked or property vandalized. Throughout the years, there has been more than one account of werewolf attacks, during which the enormous creatures break into victims' homes and maul unfortunates, whose wounds then doom them to inherit the lycanthropic curse.

Yet not all *loups-garous* are so vicious. Indeed, there are also the surprising tales of helpful werewolves—those that spend their evening hours aiding parish workers, but their unasked-for aid usually comes with a cost. Farmers who have woken to find their fields tilled will also notice that several of their chickens have been killed and eaten. Oyster fishermen have risen in the morning to find the oyster clusters they caught the day before separated into singles. While this saved them hours of hard work, roughly half the oysters were shucked and eaten.

The *loups-garous* have always come and gone as they please. Sometimes they have been known to favor a specific individual—appearing at the same window night after night, making themselves at home in a kitchen, shadowing a mark whenever he or she ventured out into the night. While some people are terrorized by this attention, others have felt comforted, believing that the creatures are actually watchful guardians rather than stalking predators.

Whatever the case, whether the *loups-garous* terrorize or protect, attack or aid, the wild creatures are all bound by common limitations. While it is said they are impervious to gunfire of any kind (ruling out the commonly held belief about silver bullets), they are reportedly terrified of frogs and are said to burst into flame if sprinkled with salt. It is also well known that the *loup-garou* can be cured of its condition if cut while in its animal form. Once blood is drawn, the werewolf is instantly transformed back to its human shape— for that one night, anyway. The cure is permanent only if the person who cut the creature tells no one the *loup-garou*'s true identity. If the secret is kept for 101 days, the werewolf is cured. If, however, the secret is revealed, not only is the afflicted lycanthrope transformed back to its canine form, but the curse is also passed on to the individual who was unable to keep quiet.

So goes the legend of the age-old *loup-garou*, the monster that was transported from the Old World to the New by superstitious French colonists. Is there any truth to the legends? Skeptics will scoff at such a question, calling the stories nothing more than dated folktales, but how many such skeptics would brave a night out on the swamps around Bayou Goula on St. John's Eve?

Run Off the Road

There is a gravel road that runs along a woodland in Calcasieu Parish. The road is nameless and infrequently traveled, though well known among those who live in the surrounding countryside. It is accepted wisdom among the locals that anyone who values self-preservation should avoid driving the road after dark.

No one has any ready explanations, but for as long as anyone can remember, strange things have been afoot on this stretch of gravel. It usually begins the same way, with expressionless figures appearing in the headlights. They are always standing completely still on the side of the road, staring blank-faced at passing motorists. The sight of these figures always fills those who see them with an inexplicable dread, and no one has ever stopped to investigate who they are or what they are doing there. It might have something to do with the way the headlights seem to shine *through* them, or with the dead expressions on their bone-white faces, but when the figures come into view, most motorists find themselves speeding up rather than slowing down.

There is never only one figure. As one fades from sight in the rearview mirror, another appears just ahead. How many are there? Seven? Eight? A dozen? Their numbers seem to vary depending on who's telling the story, but the experience always concludes in the same way: with two blazing headlights in the rearview mirror.

The lights begin as pinpoints in the distance, surely too far behind to catch up on a gravel road. And yet it soon becomes obvious that whoever is driving is moving at a great speed—almost unnaturally so. It takes no longer than a few minutes before the distant points of light are glaring in the rearview mirror. This close, the mystery vehicle turns out to be an enormous truck, and its rumbling engine is so loud it causes the ground to vibrate as it draws near.

Of course by this point, terror-stricken motorists realize that they are going to be run off the road if they don't get out of the way. Often without time to even slow down, motorists are forced to pull hard off the road as the massive truck tears by, faintly glowing with a bluish-white light and enshrouded in a strange silvery mist. Then it is gone. The night is black and silent, without even a trace of the truck's passing. Who or what is driving this ghostly truck, and why, exactly, this driver chooses to terrorize this one gravel road is anyone's guess—though by now, most locals have gotten tired of asking this question. After the sun goes down, they usually opt to let the driver have the road to himself.

The Bigfoot of Kisatchie

If, as so many cryptozoologists maintain, there is actually a Bigfoot species that has largely managed to evade human detection, then the expansive wilds of northern Louisiana would be as good a place as any for such creatures to roam. And if there's any truth to the numerous reports of large humanoid creatures in and around the lands of the Kisatchie National Forest, then it seems likely that the swamps of northern Louisiana are home to more than one such creature. Indeed, Bigfoot sightings in the region are incredibly widespread, from the Bayou Pierre in Natchitoches Parish, all the way north to Claiborne Parish, on the Arkansas border.

The Kisatchie National Forest itself is immense, divided into five separate ranger districts that are spread out over seven Parishes. A deep and abundant reserve, it is one of Louisiana's favorite destinations for outdoor enthusiasts, attracting fishers, hunters, boaters, campers and hikers, among others. Yet as crowded as the Kisatchie districts can sometimes get, it seems there are always areas where one can go to get away from everyone else. The wilderness is vast—its cypress trees, pine forests, lakes, rivers and bayous stretch out for thousands of acres. Despite all the tents, boats, four-wheelers and loggers, there are still places deep in the Kisatchie where no one treads—dark, distant places where the bayou is quiet and cypress trees are undisturbed by human hands. But it isn't human hands we're interested in.

For many years now, there have been reports of distinctly inhuman beings lurking in the swamps of the north. The region is rife with bizarre and unsettling tales invariably involving startled Louisianans and enormous, hairy bipeds

"It was standing there. I think it was looking back at me, and I just froze."

that are known to smell terrible, emit ear-splitting, hair-raising howls and leave enormous footprints in their wake. The legendary Bigfoot is hardly unique to northern Louisiana, but given the number of times the creature has been seen, the area must be practically crawling with them.

According to the Gulf Coast Bigfoot Research Organization, there have been countless sightings over the decades. In 1978, a family living near the town of Lisbon, in Claiborne Parish, was woken by a house-rattling crash in their backyard. Running to the window, they spotted the black outline of an enormous silhouette standing seven to eight feet tall. Throughout the next four years, this family witnessed other Bigfoot-related incidents, including regular high-pitched shrieks from the woods surrounding their home and the discovery of a large sleeping area within a tree hollow, covered with coarse, reeking hair. In the same region, during autumn some time in the early 1980s, a boy was hunting, perched in a deer stand when he saw a massive creature, "half-animal, half-man," crash out of the bush and stand in the open for several moments before disappearing back into the trees. Later, when the dumbstruck youngster was asked why he didn't shoot the creature, he replied: "Because it looked too human."

On November 16, 1999, another hunter described his encounter in the woods of Claiborne Parish, where, spying movement in the trees, he swung his rifle toward a large shape and took aim through his scope. What he saw through the crosshairs, however, was no deer, but a huge man-shaped figure covered in hair. Like the boy who froze in the deer stand before him, the man didn't even consider shooting.

About 100 miles south, in the Kisatchie National Forest district located in Natchitoches Parish, similar reports abound. A couple driving through a section of thick wood was suddenly overcome by a powerful smell unlike anything either of them had ever smelled. Getting out of their truck to investigate, both were seized by a disturbing, unmistakable feeling that something was watching them, something from within the trees. Wasting no time, they quickly got back into their truck and drove off, agreeing that they had come very close to something neither of them could understand.

The bordering parishes, Rapides and Sabine, have no shortage of Bigfoot lore themselves. Huge four-toed footprints covered in coarse black hair—big human shapes spotted moving quickly through the woods, signature shrieks, terrible smells, mutilated farm animals—all have been covered innumerable times by the local press, which seems ready to resurrect the possibility of Bigfoot every year or so, tirelessly reporting the latest sightings and the most recent hoaxes. For as long as there have been Bigfoot sightings, so too have there been hoaxes, and just as it is with ghosts, the Bigfoot phenomenon draws far more skeptics than believers.

Certainly, before his hunting trip in the fall of 2000, Randy German, as he shall be called for this story, would have more than likely fallen on the side of disbelief. "I don't know if I ever would've said that there was no way the Sasquatch was real," German says. "But I would've doubted it—I mean I would've really, *really* doubted it."

An avid hunter, Randy had heard his fair share of Bigfoot stories. "I suppose it always struck me as kind of strange that after all of these years, with *all* of these sightings, the only hard evidence people have ever come away with are blurry photographs and big footprints in the mud. Both of these are pretty easy to fake."

The fact that Randy German had been hunting for much of his life and hadn't caught so much as a whiff of a Bigfoot in all his expeditions into northern Louisiana only bolstered his skepticism. "I made a *lot* of trips up into them woods," he says. "They've been feeling like a home away from home for years now, and I would've liked to think that I've seen everything that walks, flies, swims and slithers through 'em." As it turned out, he was wrong. There was still one creature that the veteran hunter hadn't laid eyes on.

"I'll never forget it," German begins. "I was up in the northern part of Rapides, around the Boggy Bayou. I remember it'd been a really dry summer, and the bayou was pretty well dried up. There were all sorts of crazy stories going around in the area at that time."

Crazy stories?

Bigfoot sightings.

It began in August of that year, when a logger named Earl Whitstine claimed to have seen a huge ape-like creature about 50 yards away while he was working in the woods. Standing around seven feet tall and covered in long black hair, the creature couldn't have been too aware of how physically intimidating it was; the moment Whitstine called out to it, the thing splashed through a nearby creek and vanished into the forest.

This wouldn't be the last time the logger set eyes on the creature, however. Just two days later, the beast revealed itself to Whitstine again, around the same area. Whitstine was walking through the wooded swampland with a friend when the creature burst out of the foliage in front of them. The logger acted as he had the first time, calling out to the creature the moment it came into view. And just as it had two days previous, the beast turned and ran, this time dashing over the mud of the dried out bayou as it made its escape.

"After the loggers saw that Bigfoot the second time, the story got pretty big," German says. "The word was that they tracked the thing and found a whole bunch of footprints in the mud of the bayou. Well, the footprints were as big as you'd expect from a Bigfoot—I'm talking well over one foot long." In the wake of the sighting, Bigfoot enthusiasts converged on the area and began to spin all sorts of theories. Measuring the distance between the prints, they claimed that the creature was walking with a six-and-a-half-foot stride, far too large for a human. They found coarse black hairs around the footprints and sent them off to cryptozoologists in Oregon, who were supposed experts in Bigfoot phenomena. A local Bigfoot enthusiast came by and made casts out of the imprints in the mud. Photographs of these enormous four-toed casts were promptly printed in a local publication, the *Alexandria Daily Town Talk*, which also featured testimony from a nearby resident who claimed to have been approached by a Bigfoot while fishing in a nearby lake.

Still, Randy German wasn't impressed. "People have gotten all excited about the Bigfoot before," he says. "I remember, when I was just a kid, hearing about how they found these huge footprints in the mud in Rapides, but it turned out later that these two men'd gotten together and were having fun with a Bigfoot footprint they made out of plywood." Certainly the authorities shared German's skepticism. Wary of hoaxes, their official stance was that someone must have played a prank on Whitstine—dressing up in the guise of a Bigfoot and running off before the logger could get a better look. And the footprints? Well, as German says, all it takes is a saw and a piece of plywood.

"Much as everyone was talking about it, I don't think I gave it too much thought," German says. "I was just aiming to head up into the woods for a little alone time. I was on the lookout for deer. After I got away from Pineville and everybody making jokes about what this Whitstine guy did or didn't see, the Bigfoot didn't cross my mind much." The fact that German was planning on heading up to the same general area where the Bigfoot was sighted speaks volumes about how skeptical he really was.

"Really, me going up around Little Creek had nothing to do with the Bigfoot," he says. "I'd never been up to that part of the woods yet, so I thought this was as good a time as any. Did any of the noise about the Bigfoot being up in them parts make me think twice about what I was getting into?" German pauses, then chuckles. "Well, let me put it this way. Far as I was concerned, there's always been hunting, and there's always been Bigfoot stories. In my experience, did the two of them ever mix? Hell no."

So he set off for a few days of hunting in the backwoods he loved so much, his thoughts focused on big game and alone time rather than hairy bipeds with size 20-plus feet. Little did he know what was in store for him. "Things got right weird the first night," German recalls. "I'm a real deep sleeper. I don't toss and turn or wake up in the middle of the night unless there's a real racket going on." He knew then that something big must've happened when he found himself waking with a start.

"I wasn't sure what was going on," German says. "I knew that some big noise had just gotten me up, and that I was wide awake sitting there in my sleeping bag, but I had no clear idea what the sound was. All I had was this weird high-pitched echo going in my head, but I wasn't even sure if this was what I heard, or maybe what was left of some dream I was having." A few long moments passed with German straining his ears against the quiet of the woods. But nothing broke the oppressive quiet.

"First thing I did when I got up was take a look at my watch. It was 2:53 in the morning. I sat there and waited, just listening. The more time went by, the more I started to think that maybe a dream woke me up. My watch read 2:57 when I decided to lie back down." And yet no sooner had German's head touched the ground than a crashing noise erupted outside his tent. It sounded like bush and tree branches were being swept aside and broken. Something outside was moving, and by the sound of things, it was big, and close.

"I jumped right out of my bag right quick and was outside with my light and my gun a few seconds after that." But if German was expecting to see a prize deer in his campsite, he was disappointed. "At first, I didn't see anything," the hunter continues. "It was real quiet again, and all I had for light was this little handheld flashlight. I couldn't see anything, but there was this feeling I was getting, like there was something out there in the woods watching me, and it was making me kinda jittery."

German was scanning the treeline with his flashlight when the odor hit him. "The wind shifted and there it was," he says. "I've never smelled anything like it. It was one of the ugliest stenches I can think of. Imagine having a skunk spraying in one nostril and a dirty toe cheese in the other, and you maybe got a taste of what hit me." Then he saw it.

"I can't remember how it happened," German says. "I think I turned my face away, trying to get some air, when I saw it just past the edge of the campsite. It spooked me so much I think I shouted." He describes it as a colossal shadow standing in the cover of the trees with two wide-set eyes glowing in the darkness. "I turned the light on it and it moved," he continues. "It moved real fast, and all I really saw with the light was the upper part of its back and its shoulders. They were huge, maybe four feet wide, and completely covered with hair."

Adrenaline was running thick through Randy German's veins. There was no way he could get back to sleep, so he sat down next to a propane lantern and waited for the sun to come up. Sitting there facing the spot where he saw the creature, Randy could only stay put for so long. "I'm not saying I didn't get spooked," he says. "I was right terrified for a while, that's for sure, but the longer I sat there, the more I got my courage back. My instincts told me that the thing was long gone. Nothing that big could move around without making a hell of a racket, and I hadn't heard anything for a while. The smell was pretty well gone, too. My thinking was that if this thing got it in its head to come at me, I'd know it. You know, if I didn't hear it coming first, I'd smell it for sure." It was past four in the morning when German decided to take a look.

With his rifle in one hand and his lantern in the other, German ignored the goose bumps on his skin and crept toward the spot where the creature had been standing. "There was no doubt that the thing in the bush was what made the crashing noise. There was a mess of broken branches where the thing would've been standing and, wouldn't you guess it, a cluster of huge four-toed footprints in the dirt." German says that it was only then, as he stared down at the bewildering marks on the ground, that he reached the seemingly obvious conclusion. "I know it sounds crazy, but all that time, I wasn't even thinking Bigfoot," he admits. "Don't know if I was thinking *anything*, really. Maybe it says something about how spooked I was."

But everything changed once he was able to put a name to the thing in the dark. "It might sound weird, but as soon as I said *Bigfoot* to myself, it didn't seem so bad. I guess I liked to think that I knew what I was dealing with. Also, I'd heard a *lot* of Bigfoot stories in my time, and I'd never once heard of anyone being attacked by one of these things." And that was about all the excitement German could take for the night. It was almost five in the morning when the buzz in his veins gave way to a heavy exhaustion. Bigfoot or not, the hunter crawled back into his tent and fell asleep.

When he woke later that morning, he instantly knew that he wasn't on a hunting trip anymore. "The first thing on my mind when I woke up was that Bigfoot," he says. "I started thinking about how far it'd gone the night before, and what my chances were of getting a closer look. After an experience like that, it's hard to think about hunting deer or rabbits or whatever else—a Bigfoot isn't game, it's a *discovery*." Readjusting his gear so that he had easy access to his camera instead of his rifle, German set out that morning on an entirely different sort of hunting trip.

"I had no intention of killing a Bigfoot," he says. "What I was after was a photograph. *The* photograph. You know, to be the one who came up with final proof that these things were for real." It was an ambitious endeavor certainly, but given his recent close encounter, one that he definitely felt up for. He started that day with optimism. "I got on its trail pretty early on," German begins. "The ground was soft around my camp-site, and the footprints went on for some 30 or 40 yards, getting fainter as they went. I think I spooked the big fella when I shone the light on it, 'cause it looked like it crashed into every tree and bush that was in its way while it was running off. But it must've got its bearings soon after that. After the tracks wore off, there was almost no sign of it at all."

As he mulled over how such a large creature was able to move so quickly through the trees, German stumbled on a small animal trail. He decided to follow it, using his compass and trail markers to ensure he wouldn't get lost. "There wasn't much of a plan, when I look back on it. But with all the Bigfoot sightings that'd been going on, and what I'd just went through, I suppose my thinking was that if I looked hard enough through them woods, I was sure to find something."

His first day on the Bigfoot's trail, however, tested this confidence. "Long story short, I dragged my butt all over that forest for that whole day, seven hours or more, and nothing. I didn't find so much as one stinking hair." It was a sore and demoralized hunter who trudged back to his camp at the end of the day.

"Sometimes when you're on the hunt, patience is what you need more than anything else—and I wasn't ready to give up so easily." So it was that German spent another day wandering through the woods with hope as his only guide, keeping his eyes open for a quarry he knew nothing about. Hours passed, and he began to wonder if he was searching in vain. "It was getting pretty late in the afternoon when I decided to turn around," German says. "By that point, I was thinking about giving up. Who knew what these things' habits were? For all I could say, maybe the one I saw was halfway across the Parish by then, and I was walking around in circles for nothing."

But while he was making his way back to his campsite that second day, his hunter's patience was rewarded. "I was combing the woods for this thing for near two days, but when I finally found it, there was a second when I almost wished I didn't." It appeared without warning; German rounded a bend in the trail, and there it was.

"It was standing there, half-hidden by the trees, about 30 yards away," German says. "Big as it had looked for that second that night, it was nothing compared to the sight of it in broad daylight. It was huge. I mean, it couldn't have been less than seven feet tall, covered in pitch-black hair. It was standing there; I think it was looking back at me, and I just froze." Indeed, such a shock the Bigfoot was to German's eyes that for critical seconds, he forgot what to do with himself.

"Tell you the truth, thinking back, I'm not sure if I was stunned at the size of him, or just plain scared," he says. "Either way, I didn't move." Then the same horrendous odor he smelled the other night came over him. "It's funny. The smell of the thing snapped me out of it. All the things I'd heard about the Bigfoot came back to me. Big, hairy thing, stinks something fierce and *always* runs away at the sight of people." German stops for a few seconds before continuing. "I guess I realized what I'd been stomping around for. I had to take a picture of this thing before it bolted, right?"

Yet the moment German's hand went for his camera, the Bigfoot was gone. "To this day, when I think about it all I can do is shake my head. One second it was there, the next it was gone—so fast and so quiet that there was a second when I wondered if it was there at all." Only a second, however. The lingering stench was the only reminder he needed and, camera in hand, German took off after the fleeing creature.

"I really didn't stand a chance," German says. "This time, it left next to no trail and was making no noise either. I didn't go on after it for too long, maybe two, three minutes tops.

There was just no way I was going to catch that thing. I may as well have been running through them woods in the dark."

Thinking that he ought to head back before it actually did get dark, German turned his back on the chase and continued the trek back to his campsite. "It was a tough walk back," German says. "On one had, I was completely buzzing off the fact that I saw the thing again. Before that, I was near ready to call the whole thing off. But I was feeling sort of burned that I wasn't quick enough to snap a picture of it. All that walking around, and nothing to show for it. I was just like all the other guys who talked about seeing the Bigfoot: crazy story, but no proof."

That night, while lying in his tent, German decided he wasn't going to pursue the Bigfoot any more. "There was a part of me, a big part of me, that wanted to keep going after it," he says today. "But I thought that if I spent any more time bushwhacking for this Bigfoot, I would be crossing some kind of line. I guess I wasn't too crazy about getting all obsessed, becoming one of them bona fide Bigfoot nuts. At least *I* know what I saw. I know the truth—but all that aside, I'm glad I quit while I was ahead." German pauses and laughs. "Who knows? If I did decide to keep going after it, maybe I'd still be there today."

Whatever the case, the Bigfoot decided to give German a send off. "I was dead on my feet by the time I got back to camp," he says. "All I managed to do was heat up a can of chili and crawl into my tent. I didn't even have it in me to get out of my clothes." Collapsing onto his sleeping bag, German was one breath away from deep slumber when he was shocked awake.

"That Bigfoot must've liked me chasing it around, 'cause the noise it made that night was one of the saddest, strangest noises I've ever heard come out of any of God's creatures." Trying to describe it, German comes up with: "The sound of a woman screaming put together with a big old trumpet blast." Wide-awake again, German contemplated going out to take another look, but his body wouldn't allow it. "I just laid back down and let it go on for a bit. It let out two more of those sad honks, and that was it." German packed up and left the next morning.

"I haven't been back up there since," he says today. "There hasn't been too much talk about Bigfoots in Rapides since that year, anyway. For my part, I never told a soul about what happened during that hunting trip. You start walking around telling how you've seen a Bigfoot, and people start looking at you different. I didn't want people to start thinking of me as the crazy guy, so this is the first time I've talked about it."

Does German plan on going back up to the woods around Little Creek?

"Can't say for sure," he replies. "Maybe if somebody gets them to be a bit more socially inclined. One of those galoots still owes me a photograph."

3
Local Tales and Ghostly Memoirs

"She Was Standing by the River"

At the time of this writing, the man who experienced the following insisted that he wasn't sure whether or not to accept that he actually saw what he thought he saw one April night in 1997. And so he asked to have his real name left out of the account. We shall respect his wishes, but for the sake of the story, he shall be called Douglas Lowry.

"Since that night in New Orleans," Douglas says, "I've done a bit of reading on the way perception and psychology are connected—how what we see has a lot to do with how we're thinking. I guess you could say my hunch was right—our brains can convince our eyeballs that we're seeing all sorts of things that aren't really there."

Lowry goes on for a while on this subject, providing different examples. He brings up mirages, and how people can convince themselves they are seeing water in the middle of a desert, or how individuals grieving the loss of a loved one are often plagued by hallucinations of the recently departed. "We can convince ourselves that we're seeing all sorts of things," he says, "but knowing what is *actually* there, and what our brains have dreamed up—well, I don't know if that's such a straightforward thing anymore."

Lowry had gone to New Orleans in April 1997 to blow off some steam. He'd just completed a high-pressure work stint and decided to head out to the Crescent City to enjoy its famous amenities. "I'd been to New Orleans a few times before," he says. "A few times in college during spring break, once for Mardi Gras a few years after that. There was nothing there that was new to me. Some people, especially at my age, get shocked by the craziness of French Quarter—the all-night bars, the partying and general misbehavior on Bourbon Street. None of that stuff bothers me. I actually love to be around it, and anyway, once a guy's been to New Orleans for Mardi Gras, it's impossible to get rattled by any of that kinda stuff."

A man who thrives in an animated environment, Lowry spent his first three days in the city soaking up live music, eating well and frequenting his favorite bars. "Everything was going great—it was exactly the kind of trip that I'd needed," Lowry pauses here for a long moment before continuing, and his following words are spiced with an audible ruefulness. "But then I had to go and change the plan."

The interesting thing about New Orleans is that while it is a city famous for insouciant hedonism, there are few other places in the United States that can boast such a complex and storied culture. If there's a definite "live for the moment" manner that largely defines the city, it's also true that the weight of a dark past hangs heavily over the place. From the crowded buildings of the French Quarter to the stately old homes along St. Charles Avenue, New Orleans is a place that wears its history openly, unadorned. So many of its streets are from another time, and if one is able to tear oneself away from the burg's many gratifications, it's easy to get lost among the ghosts of New Orleans' past. It isn't called the most haunted city in the United States for nothing.

Until that April, Lowry had always limited his New Orleans forays to pleasure seeking. "Obviously, I knew something about the history and the culture. Really, it's impossible not to be aware of it when you're there, but mostly I knew about the past through the music, the jazz. Louis Armstrong and Preservation Hall and everything else."

Never giving it much thought beyond that, Lowry found himself seized by an insatiable curiosity about the place. "It started with a trip to the New Orleans Jazz Historical National Park. Next thing I knew I was getting up early to take in as many museums as I could. I hung out at the Jean Lafitte Historic Park, got up early to take a tour of the French Quarter, headed out to the Chalmette Battlefield. I guess I was hooked. I always knew that the city was full of all these great stories," Lowry says, "but I didn't really know what they were. Voodoo queens, French pirates, huge fires, jazz greats—there's a lot for a guy to wrap his head around."

Yet as Lowry immersed himself in New Orleans' past, the city began to come to life for him in a strange way. As he walked down the streets of the French Quarter, he became distracted by thoughts of the people who had lived and died there, about the stories the surrounding buildings would be able to tell if they could talk.

"That's when I started wondering about the ghosts," Lowry continues. "Everybody knows that sort of thing is a big deal in this town. There're all those cemeteries with the real old tombs. You've got the Cajuns with their werewolves and their superstitions, the voodoo from the Caribbean and all those guys and gals wearing capes in the French Quarter, pretending to be vampires. Get rid of the free candy, and pretty well every night is Halloween down there."

Though he'd never given the subject of ghosts much thought before, Lowry suddenly realized that he was intrigued by the idea. "There are tour groups taking people through the famous haunted spots all the time," he says.

Most everyone who has taken in the French Quarter at night is aware of something buzzing in the air.

"Wasn't my thing, I guess, and I have to say, the way those tour guides hammed it up, I always had problems taking the idea seriously."

But now Lowry was curious, and he promptly booked two tours: one cemetery tour in the day, and a walk through the most talked-about haunts in the French Quarter in the evening. For yet another night, he skipped the revelry in the Bourbon Street bars and went to bed early, getting a full rest for the lengthy day ahead of him.

"Looking back, I'd like to think that neither of the tours affected me that much," Lowry says. "Really, they were just run-of-the-mill ghost stories, and the tour guides were obviously putting on a show, making the accounts as dramatic as they could. What I liked about the tours was that both of them were pretty heavy into the history. I thought it was great that the legends were also little history lessons. But if you asked me if I actually *believed* in what I was hearing—no, I'd say there was no way."

And yet Lowry admits that this is merely what he'd *like* to think. "The truth was, though, that the night tour through the French Quarter actually shook me up a bit. I didn't even know it until afterwards, when I was walking back to my hotel." Lowry says that he wasn't scared per se, but was contemplative, dramatically contemplative. "I know this is going to sound really strange, but the air was buzzing that night when I was walking back to my hotel. It felt like there was definitely something up. Those buildings on either side felt like they were alive—watching. So did the shadows. Everywhere I looked, it felt like the past was looking back."

"The ghost stories," Lowry continues, "they were just stories. For all I knew they could've been true or not. That was beside the point. I wasn't even thinking about the stories I'd heard that day. I was by myself, around Ursulines and Royal, and I couldn't shake the feeling that spirits were all around me. Not just in the places that were supposed to be haunted, but all over the place: in the streets, on the balconies, rooftops, everywhere. I couldn't see them, but it was like the air was alive with them—I was walking through a city crowded with ghosts."

Many who've been to the Crescent City will agree that this isn't as crazy as it might sound. Lowry isn't the first person to walk through the French Quarter at night and be overcome by the sense that he was surrounded by ghosts. There's a reason why ghosts and the paranormal are such tourist attractions, why New Orleans carries its title, "the most haunted city in America," with a certain degree of nonchalance. Most everyone who's taken in the French Quarter at night is aware of *something* buzzing in the air. Skeptics may dismiss this *something* as the collective energy of so much liquor-soaked revelry. That was always the way Douglas Lowry looked at it—that is, until he found himself walking down Royal by himself, far away from the mania on Bourbon Street.

"I remember thinking that I just needed to get back on Bourbon, be around people, get a few drinks and everything would settle down." That was precisely what Lowry did, making his way into the manically thumping heart of the French Quarter. "Well, I ended up having quite a bit more than a few drinks," Lowry says, laughing. "I hit a few bars, and it felt good to get all the museums and the history out of my head." That's what he *thought* he was accomplishing, anyway.

"I'm not sure exactly what time it was when I decided I'd had enough. It was late—maybe two or three o'clock." Late as it was, Lowry didn't feel like going back to his hotel yet and decided to take a bit of walk before retiring. "As soon as I was back out on the street, off Bourbon, I started thinking about the city—about its past, and that feeling came back all over again. I felt like I was surrounded by ghosts."

Still, it was just a feeling. Lowry couldn't actually see anything to support the strange vibrations he was picking up. "I was a bit tipsy and really wanted to get some air before going to bed, but I have to say it was also kind of unsettling walking around the French Quarter that night. Everything felt too close, crowded, and I remember thinking I needed to get away [from] it, just for a few minutes."

With this purpose in mind, Lowry turned onto Governor Nicholls Street and headed southeast toward the Mississippi River. "I'll tell you, I was really happy to get out of the French Quarter that night," Lowry says. "Once I crossed Decatur Street and had a view of the water, the wide-open space of the Mississippi right there was a great thing. I realized then that I'd been pretty well holding my breath for the last block or two."

Breathing easy again, Lowry crossed the tracks, walked right up to the riverbank and stood there for several minutes, looking out at the river. "I still wasn't ready to go back into the French Quarter, so I went up and sat down on one of the benches along the Moon Walk," he says. "I sat there for five, maybe ten minutes, just getting my bearings. It was quiet. The whole time I was out there, only three people walked by."

Sitting with his back to the dense cluster of streets and buildings of the French Quarter, Lowry was able to pull his thoughts together. He rationalized the situation, telling himself that the combined effect of all the history he'd been soaking in, the ghost tours he'd gone on, the alcohol he'd drunk and the late hour had gotten the better of him. All he needed now was some rest. Convinced that he'd straightened everything out in his head, Lowry got up, ready to head back to the French Quarter.

"I saw her while I was turning around, of out the corner of my eye, and for a second I thought it was nothing—maybe a flash of the streetlights on the water or something. I think

I almost started walking without even bothering to look back." But he didn't. He looked back. And what he saw there, on the west bank of the Mississippi, on that dark and moonless night, almost made him yelp.

"She was standing by the river with her back to me, looking out onto the water. I could see her clearly because she was glowing, just slightly. She had a white dress that was lit up a dim bluish color, as if she was standing under a full moon. But there was no moon out. It was a black, black night, but not black enough that I wouldn't have seen this woman standing there just a second before. She was wearing this big old-fashioned white dress, and she had straight black hair," Lowry says. "I knew right away that she wasn't real. It was obvious. I mean, she showed up out of nowhere with this big old dress that no woman outside a Civil War reenactment or movie set would be caught dead in, glowing all silver and blue and making me feel like there were ice cubes falling down the back of my neck."

Fear and curiosity waged a short battle in his mind before he gathered the courage to call out. "The first time I said hello to her, she didn't move," Lowry says. "She was just standing there, still as a mannequin, looking out at the water. I waited for a few seconds, not that eager to try again. Weird as it sounds now, something about this woman was really freaking me out."

Nevertheless, he gathered his courage and tried again. "I raised my voice a bit the second time I said hello, and also asked her if she was waiting for anything, but she still didn't move." On the third attempt, however, Lowry practically shouted, and the woman moved. "It was really crazy, I mean really crazy scary to see her move. She turned around so

Still as a mannequin, she was just standing there.

slowly," he says. "It was like watching a statue turn around to look at you.

"Anyway, I may as well have been looking at a statue when she was finally facing me," Lowry continues. "This woman was as gorgeous and lifeless as any statue I'd ever seen. There was nothing in her eyes. She may have been looking right through me, but something about her seemed really, really alone. I was hit with this thought that she'd been waiting on the riverbank for a long time. She was waiting for something that never came, and she was still waiting there, even though she knew that it was never going to arrive." Lowry would never get the chance to test this hunch. Before he was able to work up the courage to ask the woman what she was waiting for, she vanished, mere seconds after she had turned to face him.

"That was it," Lowry says. "I pretty well shut off at that point. I can't say that I can remember the walk back to the hotel. I still had a couple of days before I had to leave, and I spent most of the time trying to figure out what the hell had happened. For years, I kept the incident [quiet]. Besides close friends and family, this is the first time I've spoken about it to anyone."

What is Lowry so embarrassed about? "It isn't really that I'm embarrassed," he explains. "More like uncertain. If I knew for sure that I saw what I saw, then I'd stand up and say it flat-out, 'I saw a ghost on the bank of the Mississippi River.' But looking back now, I still don't know what to think. Like I said earlier, the mind can play all sorts of tricks on you. When I think about everything that had happened leading up to that night—the ghost tours, all the history, the booze—I'm thinking it's a definite possibility that I imagined the woman in the white dress."

Or maybe he saw a ghost? "Yeah," Lowry offers, "or maybe I saw a ghost. It was New Orleans, after all. If you're going to see a ghost anywhere, it may as well be there." And yet there's more than a little disbelief in Douglas Lowry's voice. It's obvious he feels more comfortable with the psychological explanation of what he saw that night, and is still uncertain about volunteering his experience in a book of ghost stories.

Did Lowry actually see a ghost on that April 1997 night? Or was it a figment of an overworked and slightly inebriated imagination? Who knows for sure?

A Grandmother's Return

In the old district of Beauregard Town in Baton Rouge, there sits a simple house. Like many of the homes in this second oldest neighborhood of Louisiana's capital, it is bordered with cypress, bears a simple elegant porch and is accented with turned columns and intricate latticework. Nestled on a small plot of land, it's separated from neighboring homes by just a small, unassuming fence. But while it looks like any other Beauregard Town home, it isn't, really. This particular dwelling is haunted.

In Beauregard Town, houses are set close to each other. Living in close proximity to one another has fostered a deep sense of community spirit as well as a startling openness among its denizens. Walk the tree-lined boulevards, and residents will point out to an obvious stranger how many of the men for whom the streets were named were beatified through a sign-painter's error. Suddenly, St. Napoleon and St. Charles make perfect sense.

The house rests on Mayflower Street (names and locations have been changed to protect identities and privacy). Well worn, it looks very much like the late-19th century home that it is. Inside, the Bonney family goes about its daily routine. Parents Claire and Will prepare dinner as their daughters, Corinne and Jillian, watch television while pretending to study. To an outsider, it may look like a typical family scene, but there's a nearly imperceptible tension that hangs in the air. For despite the casual façade, they're all ever vigilant lest Claire's mother Helena should pop in for an unexpected and unannounced visit. The prospect of one of

Helena's visits has always been cause for a certain amount of tension. She has been dead for close to five years.

Family ties are strong in the bayous of Louisiana, and nowhere is that more true than in the Bonney home. "She died in a car accident," Corinne says when asked about her grandmother. "They said she was killed instantly. She was driving back from a visit to New Orleans in the afternoon and…" While the rest of Corinne's family learned about the tragedy from a police officer hours later, Corinne swears that she knew it the moment it happened.

"I was walking down the hall from my room," she says. "I was going to my grandmother's bedroom to get a book I'd left in there. Well, I got in there and…wow. I saw the strangest thing." A soft white glow bathed the room. "I walked in," Corinne says, her voice tinged with awe at the memory, "and all of a sudden, I was…overcome with this…incredible feeling of warmth. It was an awesome feeling. Like there was something in the room that loved me so much, and that I was totally safe there." There was an electric buzz going up and down her back, and Corinne says it took her a few seconds to realize that she was crying.

She looked around her grandmother's room then, from the bed to the dresser where all her grandmother's jewellery rested, seeking the eerie light's source. But there wasn't one. The glow seemed to come from everywhere and nowhere at the same time. And then in the middle of the room, out of thin air, a ball of light began forming before her very eyes. Somehow, as the light took shape, the room was growing darker, as if the sphere was gathering the mysterious light in the room. Corinne watched, awestruck, as it transformed itself from a vague sphere into a human figure with distinct arms and legs. The face came last. "It was my grandmother's face," Corinne says, her voice dropping slightly. "She reached out to me, and then I heard her voice inside my head.

"She said goodbye, and that I wouldn't have to worry about her anymore. She also told me to take care of my sister, and that she'd look in on me whenever she could." With those words, the vaporous figure evaporated, and Corinne was standing by herself in the dark room, wondering what had just happened. "I had no idea what to make of it. Like, did I just see my grandma's ghost? Maybe I was going crazy or something, right? I just couldn't go tell my folks about it. I didn't know what to do."

Hours later, Corinne was sitting at her desk surfing the Internet for any information she could find on the paranormal. From beyond her locked door, she heard the muffled ring of the doorbell, then her mother opening the door. Corinne heard snippets of a conversation whose small pleasantries quickly gave way to grief. When her mother began to wail, Corinne jumped from her seat and ran to the front door. She knew then what had happened. Her grandmother had indeed come to say goodbye. Her spirit had journeyed to Baton Rouge while her body was crushed between a driver's door and steering wheel on a debris-strewn stretch of highway. Corinne assumed that the eerie visit she'd received from her late grandmother would be the last. She was wrong. It was, in fact, the first of many ghostly visits from Helena that the Bonney family would experience over the years.

"You could say she's pretty much been a constant presence," Corinne says. "She's appeared to everyone in the house." Corinne then pauses before adding with a laugh,

"Even my dad, which is funny because she never really liked him too much when she was alive."

For the most part, Helena chooses to announce her presence through the usual channels: walking across the creaking floorboards of an empty hallway, turning lights on and off and playing with the kitchen taps. Her scent, a mix of tobacco and jasmine, often perfumes a corner of the sitting room. Why that particular spot? "She loved reading in that corner," Corinne recalls. "She read constantly. Sometimes, I swear I can even hear her turning the page." But every now and then, Helena manifests herself far more fully with more than just simple pranks and smells.

On the first anniversary of Helena's death, Corinne's mother, Claire, found the day almost too much to bear. She woke up on that particular morning so distressed that she chose to call in sick at work. Instead, she spent her day poring over old photo albums, peering into the face of her mother. "I don't know exactly what I was looking for," Claire says. "Maybe just something I could take from her, or maybe just how much I loved having her for a mom."

Claire had witnessed for herself the strange occurrences in the house. She recalled walking past her mother's bedroom one evening and turning on the light. After she stepped into the room, the light went out. "I thought it might have been a spent light bulb," she says. "But when I went to the switch, it was off." Still, these visits never did much to ease the pain of her loss. Never a firm believer in the paranormal, she kept trying to convince herself that the unexplained events had something to do with faulty wiring or the home's age. But on the first anniversary of her mother's death, Claire experienced something that would change her mind forever.

Unable to sleep that night, she crawled out of bed and went to the sitting room, throwing herself down on the couch, hoping that the change of location might ease her insomnia. It didn't. After another restless hour, Claire opened her eyes and stared mournfully into the darkness. "I remember thinking how much I wished I could have told her goodbye," she says. Then, out of the corner of her eye, she spotted a feeble glow. She assumed it was from the headlights of a passing car, but instead of diminishing, the glow brightened and brightened until the entire sitting room was bathed in a white light.

Claire watched, transfixed, as the figure of her mother appeared above her, hovering above the couch. The figure reached out and touched Claire's cheek. "I felt then that I had been dipped in a warm bath," she says. "All my pain just flowed away from me." Her mother didn't say anything but looked at Claire for a long moment, her eyes smiling. "I'm sure she was trying to tell me she was fine," Claire says, "and that she knows I loved her. She was trying to tell me that it was okay for me to let go now." Before Helena's spirit vanished from the room, she reached out to Claire one more time. The next thing Claire can fully remember is waking in the morning with the sensation that she had slept for ages. "I really felt like a tremendous weight had been lifted off me," Claire says. "I felt so peaceful and rested. It was incredible."

Claire's husband, Will, admits that without the help of Helena's spirit, his last wedding anniversary may have a complete disaster. "It was a big one, our 20th. I wanted to do something special. There's only so many times you can give a bouquet of roses," he says and laughs.

Still, he wasn't the most creative mind when it came to romance. He racked his brain for days but could come up with nothing more creative than the tired bouquet of red roses. "I started thinking that maybe I would get white ones that year instead," he says, laughing again. As the day approached, Will found himself sitting in the den one evening, working late, when a clatter from the bookcase caught his attention. The light from his small desk lamp was too feeble to penetrate the darkness in the rest of the room. But he smelled something altogether unusual: tobacco and jasmine.

He got up from his chair, turned on the overhead lights and walked over to the bookcase. Lying on the floor was an overturned photo album. He knelt down to pick it up. How could the album have tumbled from the shelves? Glancing around quickly, Will could see that nothing else in the room was disturbed. He grabbed the leather-bound album and turned it over. "Somehow, the album had fallen on pages where Claire and I'd pasted pictures from our first year dating," he says. "It felt like someone was trying to tell me something. And then I saw that one of the pictures was from the night that Claire and I got engaged. And yeah, I knew then that Helena was definitely up to something." The wheels began to turn in Will's mind and he conceived a plan.

For their anniversary, Will recreated the entire night on which they got engaged. They had dinner at the same restaurant, ate the same dishes and then retraced a walk they had taken so many years ago. At the end of the evening, he presented her with a picture frame, in which he'd pasted not a photograph, but ticket stubs from the first movie they'd seen together, receipts from their first dinner and programs from their first play. "Yeah, Claire was definitely surprised," Will says brightly. "She even said that I must have had help because it was everything that she'd wanted. I told her that I had. That it'd been her mother. I think she liked hearing that."

These days, Helena remains a constant presence in the Bonney home. Even when she's quiet and at rest, the Bonneys all swear that they can feel her around them. "I know she's not around anymore," Corinne says. "But, really, it doesn't feel that way. It feels as if she's here, watching us, taking care of us." The idea of a haunted house is, for many people, a frightening thing. But for the Bonneys of Beauregard Town, a haunted house is simply home.

Blood and Tears on Potter Road

Three drunken teenagers were in a car flying down Potter Road, in the town of Doyline, Webster Parish. Let us assume that these teenagers were having a good time. It was late at night. They were returning from the Doyline High School homecoming dance. They had drunk enough booze for temporary euphoria, but far too much to be driving. At the very least, it might be said they were all having great time during their final moments—the moments before they swerved off the road, crashed into a pine tree and went flying through the windshield.

That was nearly three decades ago. A black cross was put in front of the pine tree soon after the accident—a memento and a warning to the community about the dangers of drunk driving. The cross was especially effective in its purpose on the night of the homecoming dance. It began exactly one year after the accident. A group of teenagers was driving home from the homecoming dance when the black cross appeared in the headlights. Reminded of the tragedy that had occurred exactly one year ago, the teenagers got suddenly quiet, staring somberly at the grim monument as they drove by. Then one of them let out a startled shout. "Did you guys see that?"

"Did we see what?"

They stopped the car and walked over to the monument, where, illuminated by the headlights, a small rivulet of crimson was flowing from the tree to the cross. Blood. The tree was bleeding. The teenagers stood there in mute shock, watching the blood flow. And thus the legend of Potter Road was born.

Every year, on the night of the homecoming dance, someone always seemed to witness the tree bleeding into the cross. The phenomenon continued until the cross was stolen.

The Wooden Hunter

Even though he says it happened over 20 years ago, when he speaks, the uncertainty in his voice is all too clear. It's obvious he isn't comfortable talking about it, and for a moment it seems as though he may stop before he begins. If not for the promise of anonymity, he probably wouldn't be speaking at all, so he'll be known as John Mercer for the following account.

"Well, I was just a teenager, but I was still old enough to know that things weren't great. My dad just left us, and Ma was in a bit of a tough spot, no one to depend on and two snotty teenage boys on her hands on top of it. Looking back, the stuff she must've been going through—it must've been real hard on her."

Although he now admits that things must have been tough on the recently single mother, John and his elder brother, Lucien (also an assumed name), were in their mid-teens at the time, and were too absorbed in their own worlds to give their mother's plight too much thought. Until, that is, their mother turned around and changed their worlds completely.

"I'd turned 14 that year," John begins, "when Ma told us we were moving out around Lafayette." It was a big move. Until then, the Mercers had lived in the same house since his brother was born. He'd had the same friends his entire life, felt right at home in his neighborhood and had a massive collection of model airplanes that he knew would be next-to-impossible to transport.

"I was a complete airplane freak," John says. "I spent pretty well every cent I had on those damn kits. My room was stuffed to the gills with every kind of plastic airplane you could think of—if it had guns and wings, chances are I'd glued it together and hung it up in my room." Having difficulty seeing past his adolescent obsession, John's biggest concern as the move loomed closer was that his model airplanes must survive without a scratch. With the single-minded determination reserved for resolved teenagers, he convinced his mother that his models ought to be packed and moved apart from all their other possessions.

And so two days before the real move began, John had all of his models carefully packed away and ready to go. "Ma wasn't having anything to do with this foolishness herself, but she lent my brother her car and made him drive me out to the new place."

The house wasn't new but was an old two-story place that had been renovated after a fire had damaged much of it just a few years previous. Neither of the brothers were all that interested in the details of the place when they pulled up to it for the first time with a trunk full of plastic airplanes. John was preoccupied with making sure all of his airplanes were going to survive the move; Lucien was busy trying to look as miserable as possible. "I wasn't too thrilled about the move, but my brother was downright sour about it. He was always the popular kid in school. Good at sports, always had a girlfriend. Switching schools and moving so far from our friends really got to him. He couldn't have been too thrilled, either, that he had to kill a day helping his little brother move his models."

All their dramas aside, it was during this first trip to the house that the brothers got the first hint that bizarre things were afoot there. John continues: "There wasn't a single thing in the house—we hadn't moved one box in yet. Me and my brother went up to my room loaded with boxes. I remember I was in front of him, and was the first guy in my room. I just walked across and was putting my box down on the floor when I heard him say, 'What the hell is that?'"

Turning around, John's gaze went from Lucien, who was standing at the doorway, to the thing he was staring agape at. On the floor right in the middle of the room was a small wooden statuette, standing no more than four inches tall. "I'm not sure what was weirder," John says, "that I walked into a completely empty room and didn't notice this thing standing there, or the way my brother looked. It was just this little wooden man, but the way Lucien looked—he looked really creeped out."

John walked over and picked up the little statuette. It was a hand-carved man in old colonial dress leaning on a musket rifle, the detail of its legs blending into an uncarved wooden base. "There was no way to know for sure, but I had a feeling that this thing was real old. I started thinking that maybe it was worth some money and maybe we should save it."

When he told Lucien this, his big brother snapped out of his quiet apprehension. "He laughed at me and said something about how it probably just belonged to some stupid kid that lived in the house before us. Said it was probably his name on the thing." Still, John goes on to say that he didn't really buy what his brother was saying, and that something about the little wooden man that bothered him. "I wasn't sure what to think. All I can say for sure was that the weight of it in my hands made me think that maybe it was rare, and the longer I thought about it, the more I knew there was no way it was there when I first walked across the room."

Strange as the statue was, there was still a trunk full of airplane models to move. "My brother told me to forget about that thing, and I put it down against the corner." Going back out to the car, they proceeded to unload the trunk. "By the time we were done, we'd almost forgotten about that weird little wooden guy. Before we left, though, my brother picked him up and put him on the kitchen counter. I still don't know whey he did that."

The boys weren't the only ones struck by the oddness of the statuette. Over the next few days, as their mother joined in the moving, she commented on the wooden man numerous times. "I could tell that Ma, just like my brother, was kind of freaked out by him." According to John, she was always conscious of the wooden man standing there on the kitchen counter. Even in the ensuing days, as boxes began piling into the new home and all the family's possessions were in complete disarray, she always seemed to have one eye on him. "She was getting aggravated, I could tell, until she finally just took the statue and shoved it behind a box, just to get it out of her sight," John recalls. "Wouldn't you know it, it showed up on top of that very same box the next day."

After that, John's mother grew more perturbed about the statuette than his brother. She tossed it in the garbage. When he reappeared on the kitchen counter later on that day, still staring stoically, resting on his musket, John's mother confronted her boys. "She was definitely upset," John says. "She told us that the wooden statue didn't belong to us, and that it was probably left behind by whoever lived in the house before. And that she didn't want other people's garbage in her new home." The boys tried to tell their mother that they hadn't touched him, but she refused to listen. She threw it away again, this time making sure it was buried deep in the trash-can. When it showed up on the kitchen counter again the following day, John's mom she decided she'd had enough. She threw the little statue of the hunter in the backyard fire pit and incinerated it.

Though the statuette was never seen again, it quickly became evident to the Mercer family that the statuette wasn't the only queer thing about their new home. "It got real weird real quick," John says. "If you left a door open, chances are it was shut you when you got back. Same thing if you closed a door behind you. Come back a few minutes later and it's wide open. At night, Ma said she heard music playing real low, even though me and my brother would be sleeping, and the television and stereo were turned off."

Yet as far as John was concerned, what was even stranger than these occurrences was his mother's reaction to them. After her jittery response to the wooden statuette, she was able to cope quite well with whatever was in the house. In fact, she grew to *like* the presence, to take comfort in it. His mother experienced a warm comfortable feeling whenever she got the sense that the mysterious presence was in the room. "Maybe it made her feel less alone," John says. "It was right after her divorce. She had a lot on her plate, and no one to share it with. Weird as it sounds, I think she felt safe that there was someone besides her boys in the house."

The same could not be said for John's brother, however. "My brother never did get use to that house," he recalls. "From the start, he was the one who got the worst deal from that move. He had a lot of real good friends in our old neighborhood, was really attached. He would've hated the new place just on account of it not being the old neighborhood.

But the stuff that was happening there freaked him out the most. He could never get comfortable in that house." While John's mother felt comforted by the sense that she was being watched over by friendly eyes, his brother felt a vague threat—like whatever was watching him didn't really like him.

There were times when John's mother and brother felt the presence at the same time, while sitting in the same room. "That was always a funny thing to see," John says. "Ma would be sitting there reading a book, and my brother would be watching TV or something. Then, out of the blue, he'd start groaning about how cold it was in the room. He'd be getting all fidgety and grouchy—glare at me and Ma. Meanwhile, Ma would be sitting in her reading chair, snug as a bug in a rug. A minute would pass, maybe two, then we'd hear footsteps in the room, or else a real quiet chuckle. My brother wouldn't sit there too long after that. Ma would always get up and try to calm him down, but he didn't want to talk about it at all." These sorts of events continued on for nearly a month, and Lucien took to spending as little time in the house as possible. If no one was at home, he would refuse to go inside. It wasn't an uncommon thing for John to come home to find his brother outside, waiting for either him or his mother to arrive before going inside.

"It was getting worse and worse for him every day," John says. "And things were getting bad between him and Ma." The problem was that John's mother couldn't see how the same presence that made her feel so secure and comfortable was able to have such a negative effect on her son. At first she thought it was all in his head, that all he needed to do was accept the presence and it wouldn't be so bad anymore. When it became apparent that this wasn't going to happen, she began blaming him, accusing her son of playing the situation up because he wanted to move back to the old neighborhood. And there was no way that was going to happen.

"The mood in our place was getting pretty ugly," John says. "Between the divorce, Ma, my brother and this invisible thing that was always padding around, it was a dysfunctional three-ring circus." If so, the circus left town after just over a month, when the ringmaster finally decided enough was enough.

"To this day, my brother won't talk about what happened," John says. "I don't know if it was something he saw or something he heard, but whatever it was, it must've been nuts. In all my life, and ever since, I'd never heard my brother scream like that."

It was past midnight on a school night when John and his mother were wakened by a spine-chilling screech. "I thought at first that it was the thing in the house that made that noise, because it didn't sound anything like my brother. He was always one of those quieter type of guys. He gets angry, but you never hear him yell at anyone. Never raises his voice." John stops for a moment before continuing. "Well, this yell was so loud it made me jump clean out of bed."

Throwing open his door, John stepped out just in time to see his brother tear down the hallway, his eyes wide in horror. "Ma was out of her room right then, too," he says, "yelling about what the hell was going on."

Neither of them would ever find out, but that was it for the Mercers in their new home. They moved out at the end of that month. "It was a hard thing for Ma. She really liked it there, and she must've been really looking forward to getting settled and getting on with her life. But you know," John says, pausing for a moment, "it was also good to know that no matter how much she felt at home in a place, she'd move out of it if her boys couldn't deal with it."

John, however, was forced to repack and transport all of his model airplanes, and was nowhere near as understanding.

Haunting in Baton Rouge

"The place looked fine when I saw it in the afternoon, but my first night there, I knew there was someone else living in it." Jean McClusky (an assumed name) had just moved into an apartment suite and was about to discover some rather unsettling things about his new home. "At first glance, there was nothing too special about it. It was a basic apartment—one bedroom, pretty cheap. Didn't really give it too much thought. My old roommate was getting together with his girl, and this had been her place before. We just traded. I moved in quick, no fuss."

As McClusky says, however, he'd only ever seen the apartment suite in the afternoon. Everything changed when the sun went down. "I remember feeling it even when I had my pals over. There were three guys who helped me move, and we were sitting around, having pizza and beer on the boxes. Then it was like, *bang*, out of nowhere—this jolt hit me, and I knew for sure that we weren't the only ones in there."

As sure as he was, McClusky kept the news to himself. "Truth is, I've been tuned in to this sort of thing all my life," says the Louisiana native. "I've known ghosts exist since I was four years old." He recalls his first childhood memory: lying in bed, about to fall asleep, and noticing the light in the hall flickering on and off under the door. He says that was the first time he experienced the "*I'm not alone*" sensation that has come over him so many times throughout his life. In the next moment, the door swung open and he found himself looking at a little girl standing in the doorway, silhouetted by the lights that continued to flash on and off behind her. "I was sure the second I saw her that she was different from me and my parents and everybody else I knew," McClusky says. "I knew right away that she was actually a ghost, and it probably sounds hard to believe, but I wasn't scared by it either."

He goes on to say that the girl stood there for a few minutes before vanishing, turning off the light in the hall as she left. "After that, I started seeing this girl around quite a bit," McClusky says. "She showed up everywhere: at the breakfast table, in the backyard, when I was in my room. She never said anything to me, and no one else could see her, but I knew she was real. Yeah, she was dead, but she was also real."

McClusky says that he's long gotten used to the spirits of the dead visiting him. Though he's never been able to communicate with them, he is very frequently aware that they're present. "They're just *there*. Usually, they don't do much of anything. I've heard a lot about how ghosts can be vengeful or really pissed off about something. But I've never gotten that with the spirits I've seen. If they are pissed off, they aren't telling me about it. In fact, in all my years they've never said a word at all."

And for his part, McClusky learned not to say anything about them. "Growin' up, I picked up right quick that it wasn't smart for me to be walking around telling people that I was seeing dead people. I tried it out on a few friends early on and learned that if I didn't want to be the freak in the room, it was best to keep it to myself."

So McClusky didn't say a word when the feeling came over him as he sat in his new apartment, having pizza and beer with the friends who had helped him move. "No way those dudes could've known it, but there was a dead person in the room with us. I couldn't see him yet, but I had a hunch that he'd show up sooner or later—just a matter of time."

The feeling didn't subside, but only grew stronger when his friends left. But even then, no spirit revealed itself to the new tenant, and he busied himself unpacking boxes.

"The buzz was getting stronger and stronger. I knew I wasn't alone in there, but the spirit that was in there wasn't showing up. The feeling was getting real strong, though. Like I *knew* he was there with me. I was so sure of it I could *almost* see him, if that makes any sense, but he just wasn't showing. After a bit, I got to thinking that maybe he was shy or unhappy that I was there."

In all the years he had lived among ghosts, this was the first time that he ever got the suspicion that a spirit wasn't happy with him. "I can't really say *how* I knew, but I was sure that the ghost was a man. I knew right away when I first got the feeling that he was there. And I started to wonder if this guy was mad at me.

"Now, I've never really had much luck trying to get them to talk," McClusky continues, "so my way of thinking has been 'they don't talk to me, I don't talk to them.' It always worked for me fine." Yet on this night, as the inexplicable tension in the apartment seemed to mount with every passing minute, McClusky felt inclined to communicate.

"I felt a bit dumb about it," he says, "but I ended up talking to the air in the kitchen. I started saying that I knew he was there, that I had seen ghosts my whole life, and that I was getting the feeling he wasn't too happy. I asked him if there was anything that he wanted to say, or anything I could do to make him feel better about me moving in. I went on for a bit, but there was no answer. Just that weird feeling, sort of like an adrenaline buzz, like there was somebody in the room who wanted to hit me."

Disturbed as he was by the presence, McClusky was also determined not to let it get in the way of what he had to do, and he continued unpacking until it was time to go to sleep. Yet while he was able to keep the presence from disturbing his work, he wasn't as successful in keeping it from interrupting his sleep. "I woke up that night to the sound of water running," McClusky says. "I wasn't really sure what was happening at first. It was loud. It sounded like every tap was opened all the way."

Taking a second to shake off the grogginess, McClusky practically jumped out of his skin at the sight of the figure standing at the foot of his bed. "That right scared me. I've been seeing ghosts almost my whole life, but that bugger really caught me off my guard." Sitting up quickly, he reached for his lamp to get a better look at the figure, but in his haste, he knocked the lamp off his night table. "There I was, swearing away, looking at this guy standing at my bed, scrambling for the lamp and wondering if this son of a gun is flooding my place, when the light went on all by itself!"

The man at the foot of the bed vanished almost the moment the lights went on, but McClusky was still able to get a good look at him. "He was a bigger fella—dressed in plain gray. I remember his face: he had dark hair and a thick neck, and the way he was standing there, arms crossed over his chest, he looked unhappy as hell." McClusky jumped out of bed as soon as the man blinked out of sight, and he made his way to the bathroom and kitchen, where, as he suspected, every tap in the apartment suite had been turned on. Thus began the ordeal in his new apartment.

"I really didn't know what to do," he continues. "I'd been seeing ghosts forever but, you know, I'd never really been *haunted* by one. We always got along fine. None of 'em had ever gotten on my back. But this guy, he couldn't get enough of me. He just wouldn't let it rest. Every day it was something else."

McClusky describes coming home from work one day to find all of his recently unpacked videotapes put back in their boxes. On another occasion, every cupboard and drawer in the kitchen was opened, with their contents—pots, pans, plates, bowls, cutlery—strewn over the counter and the floor. The buzzer would frequently sound in the middle of the night, even though there was nobody there. He'd hear an angry male voice whispering a litany of unintelligible whispers when he was trying to get to sleep. "You name it, it was going on," he laughs. "It was like I stepped into a horror movie or something, real 'I see dead people' kind of drama, if you know what I'm saying."

The Louisianan is able to laugh about it now, but he admits that the constant mischief was driving him to wits' end. "After about a week of this, I was over at my pal's place, the guy I lived with before, whose girlfriend used to live in the apartment I was in," McClusky says. "I wasn't sure how to go about asking, so I just asked her if she'd ever dealt with any crazy stuff when she lived there."

"My pal's a bit of smart ass, and just like I expected, he made some crack, but what his girlfriend said was a surprise. She gave me this serious look and said how it was weird, but she never felt alone when she was living in the apartment. But it wasn't a bad thing. She said always felt safe there, like there was someone watching over her and making sure that she was okay. She said something about how she never believed in guardian angels or anything like that, but after living in the apartment for a few years, she wasn't so sure anymore."

Her testimony explained a lot, but it wasn't until two days later, when McClusky had his former roommate and his girlfriend over for beer, that he figured out the problem with his resident ghost. "We were in the living room, drinking and watching TV, when I got hit with the feeling that he was coming," McClusky remembers. "But this time, the feeling was different. It didn't have that angry edge. It wasn't giving me that jumpy adrenaline rush."

Looking over to where the couple was sitting on the couch, McClusky started in surprise. There, sitting close to his friend's girlfriend, was the same figure that had stood at his bed a week ago. The couple was oblivious to the heavyset man, but was amused at the reaction of their friend. "Yeah, my pal's like, 'you alright, man? You look like you've just seen a…'" he interrupts himself with a laugh before continuing. "I don't need to finish it, right?"

"Well, after they left, things quieted down at the apartment for a while. And when it started it to get a bit frosty again, I invited them over for some food. That seemed to keep him happy; as long as he gets to see my pal's girl from time to time, everything is cool. Not too long ago, I got a photo in the mail of both of them on a beach in Mexico," he continues. "Little postcard from this vacation they're on. First thing I did was put that shot up on the fridge. I like to think it keeps the guy I'm living with happy. Here I was thinking that it was something personal about me. He's just got a bit of a crush, that's all."

If this is truly the case, the next residents of the apartment better hope McClusky keeps the photo of the couple on the fridge when he decides to move out.

A Spirit in the Woods?

"My girlfriend and I were driving down from El Dorado, Arkansas," Matthew Hyatt begins. "We crossed into Louisiana on the 558 and were looking for a place to camp that night. We didn't plan it or anything," he says, "but the Lake D'Arbonne State Park was right there, so we thought, 'sure.'"

The couple was nearing the halfway point of their cross-country road trip from New York City to New Orleans and back again. They had packed all their camping equipment with them and opted to pitch a tent over staying in motels whenever the opportunity presented itself, so neither were daunted by the prospect of spending the night outdoors. They actually preferred it. It was the first time in Louisiana for both of them, and as was usually the case on their first night in a new state, they were both in high spirits.

"The park was great," Matthew continues. "We drove in around afternoon and had a great campsite that was just a few minutes walk to the lake. There weren't too many people. It was nice and quiet, and I remember we were both totally amped camping there that night and being so close to the end of our trip." To celebrate their arrival in the Creole State, the couple tried approximating a jambalaya for supper, frying up some sausage and beans with rice and too much hot sauce. Then they took a dip in the lake. Matthew laughs. "I know it sounds like I'm raving here, but that was such a great night. I mean, there was some real good energy happening."

Hoping to keep whatever it was going for as long as they could, the couple decided to go for a walk in the woods. "By then, the sun was starting to go down, so we took our flashlights with us." A young couple heading out into the woods for a night time hike—Matthew is quick to point out how the scenario sounds like the set-up for a slasher movie.

"I know, I know," he laughs. "*Friday the 13th,* right? *Sleepaway Camp.* Believe me, I was getting some good mileage out of it—running ahead and hiding behind trees, breathing heavy. Lots of fun, for me at least. My girlfriend was getting a bit annoyed. But in a sort of semi-amused way, I'd like to think."

The semi-amusement lasted for about half an hour or so, until Matthew saw the shape in the trees. "It was pretty dark by then," he says. "We were on a pretty wide trail though, and getting back to our site wasn't a problem. I wasn't thinking about turning around yet, and I'm pretty sure my girlfriend wasn't either. But then things got weird."

Matthew was a few yards ahead of his girlfriend, hiding behind a stand of trees and playing at pretending to startle her, when he heard movement in the woods behind him. "I got that kind of rush you get when you know there's an animal nearby," Matthew says. "No big deal. I wasn't freaked out or anything. I turned around with my flashlight, thinking maybe there was a possum there, or a raccoon or something."

Hardly a possum or a raccoon, the sight that greeted him when he turned around made his jaw drop. "It's still hard to describe it," he says. "It was deeper in the woods, behind a lot of trees, so it wasn't like I had a clear view of it. But it kind of looked like a human figure—I could make out two legs, a head, neck and arms—or more like an *outline* of a human figure." He pauses. "This is gonna sound weird for sure, but maybe even a shadow of a human figure, with no body around to cast that shadow."

Matthew quickly adds that he was standing some distance away from the figure, and that he cannot say for certain whether he couldn't make out any distinctive features in the outline because of the dark and the distance, or if there really were no actual features to make out. "You know, it probably wouldn't have gotten to me the way it did if it was just the figure," he says. "I probably would've just assumed it was some guy out walking around by himself."

Yet it was more than just a shadowy figure moving in the woods. "The way I felt, though, when I saw this thing—I know this is something people always say when they talk about seeing ghosts and stuff—but the *hairs* on my *neck*, they weren't just standing up. They were doing the can-can! I could feel chills going up my back, then back down, then up again. On one hand, my mind was really curious about what I was seeing, and I was trying to look harder. I wasn't really scared or anything, I was just trying to see what it *was*. But then on the other hand, my body was totally terrified. I sort of felt like, with the goose bumps and all, my body knew something my mind didn't—if that makes any sense."

And what did Matthew's body know? What was it trying to tell his mind? Apparently, whatever it was, his girlfriend's body was telling her mind the same thing. Matthew was standing there, looking into the trees for no more than several seconds when he heard his girlfriend shout his name. "Her voice sounded scared, and that snapped me out of it," he says. "She was calling for me, saying: 'Matt, is that you?'"

Instantly stepping out of the woods onto the trail, Matthew called back, reassuring her that it was him in the trees. But as he approached her in the rapidly fading light, he could see that she wasn't looking at him, but staring transfixed at the approximate location where he had seen the shadow moving. "She had this look on her face that I'd never seen before," he says. "Partly freaked out, but also totally fascinated. I could tell that she was as curious as I was about what was in there."

Matt asked his girlfriend what she had just seen. "The only thing she said was, 'I saw something moving in the trees.' But I could tell by how she was acting that there was more to it than that. She was freaked out, too. Whatever was out there, it got to her the same as it got to me."

For several moments, they stood there in silence, both looking hard into the trees, trying to spot the moving shadow in the rapidly darkening wood. "We lost him," Matthew says. "Both of us had seen him less than a minute before, but now he was gone. Or probably not gone, right? But *hidden*. Really, how do you spot a shadow in a forest at night? The trees were full of shadows."

Matthew's girlfriend was the one who broke the silence, telling him then what she thought she saw: "a moving shadow." And according to Matthew she was relieved to hear that he saw the same thing. "So neither of us was crazy," Matthew laughs. "That was a bit of a relief. But now we were standing there looking at each other, wondering, 'Now what?'"

Matthew claims that one of the things he and his girlfriend have in common is a sense of adventure. "A lot of people would probably be in a big rush to get out of there," he says, "but my girlfriend gave me this look. It's crazy, but there was a part of her that was getting such a thrill out of this. She was looking at me thinking, 'Can you believe this!? There's some crazy shadow thing out there! Isn't this great?'

The funny thing is, I totally got it. My heart was going like crazy. I just kept asking myself the same two questions, over and over: *What was out there? Did I see a ghost?*"

However adventurous they both might be, neither Matthew nor his girlfriend was ready to go wandering into the woods in the pitch dark. "By that point, it was getting late, and we decided to turn around. My girlfriend said something about sitting around by the lake for a while before we called it a night."

As they walked, there was just one topic of conversation. "We were going back and forth about what we saw, talking a bit too loud," Matthew says. "I think both of us were a bit rattled. Not just with the shadow we saw. The night seemed a little bit different going back. I kept looking at the edge of the light from the corner of my eyes, thinking for sure that something was out there, watching. So anyway, maybe the talking made it less spooky." Then, in the time it took for a twig to snap, the talking trick stopped working.

"There was a noise in the trees, and I started feeling that chill again," Matthew says. "Our chatter stopped so fast. And even though she didn't say anything, I could tell by my girlfriend's face that she was feeling the same thing." When the rustling sounded again, Matthew spoke up.

"We'd both slowed down and were listening hard when I thought I'd say something." Matthew sent a tentative 'hello' out into the darkness, but no response came back. "There was some more noise, and we both stopped to hear better. We were shining our lights in the direction of the sound, but we still couldn't see anything."

That was when Matthew's girlfriend decided she was more spooked than thrilled by the weirdness in the woods.

"She pretty well had it at that point," Matthew says. "She told me she was through messing around and wanted to get back to our campsite. I didn't think it was a bad idea either, so we picked up the pace down the trail."

They were walking fast, minds set on getting back as quickly as possible without actually running, and they might have made it if the clouds hadn't shifted then, flooding the forest with moonlight. "There was a full moon out that night, but the night was dark with all the clouds. When it cleared, everything lit up so brightly. It was incredible. Our shadows were out, and we could see into the trees on both sides."

Seconds later, Matthew practically jumped out of his skin when his girlfriend let out a startled scream. "She didn't have to say anything," he says. "I didn't see what made her scream, but I knew what it was. We both started running at the same time." Looking over his shoulder as he ran, he saw it—the humanoid shadow in the woods, pitch black against the dark blue moonlit night. It was the clearest view he had seen of it, and it did indeed appear to be a walking shadow, lacking any physical form whatsoever. It wasn't moving, but simply standing at the edge of the woods, right against the trail, several feet from where they had been standing. He realized his girlfriend must have looked over to see it right next to her.

"We didn't stop running until we got to our campsite," Matthew continues. "We were so frazzled by that point that we were laughing—laughing hard for I don't know how long. After that, we got into our tent. We were still frazzled, and stayed up whispering about what it could've been, listening at the same time for what was outside." Hushed by the slightest sound, but resuming their speculation after a few more moments, the couple continued like this until they eventually fell asleep. When they awoke under the blue sky of a brilliant morning, the events from the night before seemed like a dream.

"It was a really nice place, and we ended up staying there for two more nights," Matthew says. They spent their days taking it easy: killing time on the lake, walking around the woods. They even ventured back to where they saw the shadow at dusk, but there was no repeat occurrence. "By the time we left, we were both sort of unsure about what happened that night," he says, "We saw what we saw, but the more time went by, it felt too weird to be real. It had us wondering if maybe it was a trick of the light, or maybe some other camper fooling around, trying to scare people. I don't know." When Matthew embarks upon such explanations, however, his voice hesitates. "All I can say for sure is that if somebody was fooling with us, he did a damn good job. Because since then, I've spent some time thinking about stuff I've never really thought about before—about ghosts and spirits and things that might be there, but that maybe we can't see."

Was there actually something supernatural watching Matthew and his girlfriend in the woods around Lake D'Arbonne? Or was it indeed a trick of the light or someone fooling around? Though Matthew goes through the trouble of offering his rational explanations after the fact, the obvious uncertainty in his voice makes it all too clear what *he* really believes.

Murder in the Red Barn

Highway 810. A short stretch of road, less than 10 miles long, runs east-west along the southern shore of Craney Creek Lake, connecting SH 4 and SH 34. Most motorists taking 810 don't have much cause to consider the road they're on. Perhaps they're vacationers looking for a place to camp on the lake. Maybe they're just commuting between Jonesboro and Chatham. They could be lost. Or…they could be looking for the red barn.

Not that one needs to be looking for it to notice it. Appearing off to the side of the 810, the big barn has a way of drawing people's attention. Suddenly uncomfortable travelers often remark at the sight, at the air of foreboding that hangs over the barn. Some don't remark on it at all, but step on the gas, anxious to put the vaguely sinister building behind them. And then there are those who slow down and pull over.

Mostly, they're local teenagers looking for excitement. The weird phenomenon that is said to occur on the trail by the barn has been talked about for some time. For decades, teenagers have waited until dusk and made the drive down the 810, turning off by the red barn and parking their cars on the nearby trail. The trail leads into the woods, but no one need get out of the car, for after exactly 15 minutes, a hard rapping sounds on the windshield. The knocking is always the same: hard and desperate, as though someone is pleading for help, begging to be let in. But there is never anyone there—only the trees illuminated by the headlights, and the red barn looming behind.

Though no one is able to verify it, legend has it that many years ago, a lone black man was lynched inside the barn then and hung up on one of the meat hooks suspended from the rafters. While the frantic knocking may very well be his spirit begging for escape, no one ever sticks around long enough to find out. Invariably, amid terrified yells and excited shouts, engines are started and cars peel off back onto the highway, the haunted barn fading out of sight in the red glow of the taillights.

An Uptown Haunting

Among people who study such things, it is generally accepted that the city of New Orleans is thick with ghosts. More than one paranormal authority has dubbed it "the most haunted city in America." And it has become so accepted as such that the city's supernatural legends have become a significant tourist attraction. Yet when people speak of the ghosts of New Orleans, the usual assumption is that they're talking about the French Quarter. This is where the city finds its provenance; this is where the great bulk of its rich and troubled history played out; this is where its human drama and misery have left their psychic imprints. In short, this is where the ghosts are.

But not all the ghosts. Crossing Canal Street, one leaves the cramped and magical bustle of the French Quarter behind. There, the outgrowth of old New Orleans stretches into the new—the modern office buildings between Canal and Howard, the dark brick buildings of the Warehouse District, the highways and expressways and the crowded traffic that moves along them. Anyone getting on the St. Charles Avenue streetcar will pass through such generic urban scenes, until the car crosses Jackson Avenue. There begins the city's historic Garden District, where recently arriving American residents built their community after the construction of the New Orleans and Carrollton Railroad in the 1830s.

A cultural counterpoint to the dense Creole settlement of the Vieux Carre, the Garden District is filled with row upon row of opulent houses situated along grand oak-lined streets. This is where the English-speaking merchant class lived, not welcomed by or willing to mix with the Creoles crammed against the bend in the Mississippi. The supernatural legends of the French Quarter—so storied and plentiful—are gregarious, spilling out of the buildings, mixing with the living, freely letting the public in on their most gruesome and disgraceful details. The ghosts of the Garden District, however, are something else all together.

With each house standing singular and apart, there is a sense of reserve here that is wholly lacking in the Vieux Carre. Here, the curtained windows of pillared manors keep secrets that passersby can only wonder at. While one may sense that many of the grand old houses along these uptown streets have stories of their own to tell, there is also the sense that they would rather keep these stories to themselves.

Certainly, the woman who came forward to disclose this uptown haunting knows all about reluctance to air one's personal ghosts, and she agrees to tell her story only on condition of anonymity. She shall be called Maggie Davis for the purposes of this story.

"We've had this house in the family for a long, long time," she begins, "for 100 years and more. The things that have been going on here go back just as far."

Davis insists on keeping the street name of the house to herself, and she only reveals that her family home is modest by Garden District standards, tall and narrow and definitely looking its age. Worn and creaky for as long as she can remember, the Garden District house has been a constant in Davis' long life—as has the spirit that resides there. "One of my earliest memories is my ma telling me about her," Davis says. "She said that there was somebody else living with us in our house. She said it was a girl, a little girl that didn't mean any harm to no one but could cause a little bit of trouble from time to time."

Davis explains that she got the talk after going up to her room one day and finding her toy chest open with all its contents flung about the room. "I was really upset about this, you see," she explains. "I had an older brother who tormented me constantly, and I was convinced that it was him." After running downstairs and telling her mother about the mess in her room, she expected a promise that her brother would be punished. Instead, her mother told her that her brother had been outside playing the entire day. There was no way he could be responsible for the mess.

"That was when she told me I wasn't the only little girl living in our house," Davis says. "There was another girl. No one could see her, but she had lived here for a long time, as far back as when my ma was a little girl. My ma told me that this little girl liked dolls, and she thought maybe it made her upset that I hid all my dolls in my chest." After that, Davis made a point to keep her dolls out on her dresser, and her room was never ransacked again.

This isn't to say that the invisible resident left Davis alone. At a very young age, she learned to notice small signs of the spirit's presence. "Sometimes I'd come back to my room and know that the girl was there because my dolls would be put on my dresser in a different order," Davis says. "She liked to play around with my dresses, too. A lot of the time my wardrobe door was left open. Whenever she was mucking around in there, she left my clothes hanging improperly or else on the floor."

In other instances, Davis would walk into her room to find a number of her possessions hovering in midair.

"I remember there was one time when I opened the door and my brush was floating around all by itself, without anybody holding it," Davis laughs. "I was a rather capricious little thing, and shouted at it to let my brush go. I shouted that it was *my* brush, not hers." No sooner had she shouted this than the brush dropped to the floor. On other occasions, she caught pillows, clothes and blankets drifting through the air on their own. They dropped to the floor moments after she entered her room.

"We had a complicated relationship, this girl and I," Davis continues. "Sometimes she really upset me. It really bothered me that she would go through my stuff whenever she wanted. I didn't have a choice. I had to share my dolls with her, and whenever she made a mess, I was the one who had to clean it up. But when it came to my brother, we were both on the same side."

When she was a child, Davis was in a state of virtual war with her elder brother. In this struggle, the mysterious "girl" who usually infuriated her so much was her ally. "My brother and I used to get into awful rows, and she was always on my side," Davis says. "If I was outside the house, I was on my own, but inside, almost anything that boy did to me, he'd pay for it one way or another." According to Davis, if her brother ever got too carried away with the name-calling, he would feel an ice-cold hand smack him across the back of the head. More than once, he burst into her room with the intent of destroying some of her dolls. But he never made it more than two steps past the threshold before an invisible force swept his legs out from under him, causing him to go tumbling to the floor. He would get back up to continue into the room, but could never take another step before being knocked back down.

"He grew up to be fine," Davis says with a laugh, "but, oh, that brother of mine loved to torment me. I don't know what I would've done if it wasn't for my invisible friend. She forced him to behave, when we were in the house, anyway. He learned that lesson pretty quickly. There was a price to pay whenever he was cruel to his little sister." Most of the time, the retaliation was immediate, but Davis goes on to say that her brother suffered more than one sleepless night for the things he had done during the day. "She really got him scared when she came into his room at night," Davis says. "It only happened a few times, but each time he told my ma about it. [The girl] would open up his door and walk in. He couldn't see her, but he could hear her footsteps on his floor. She walked right up to his bed and whispered to him that she saw what he had done that day and she wouldn't let him be mean to me."

Of course, it didn't take many such visits to get Davis' brother to behave himself around his sister. His mother told him, as she had told Maggie, that the house was inhabited by the ghost of a girl who, apparently, had a fair bit of sympathy for his waylaid sister. The story was enough to leave his sister in peace. This tenuous civility, however, only lasted when they were in the house. Davis soon learned that her brother's hostility only worsened when it was pent up, and the bullying increased when she was outside. "You could say I spent a lot of time indoors when I was a young," Davis laughs. In that time, she grew accustomed to the presence in the house.

"I stopped being grumpy about sharing my things with her," Davis says. "I took to talking to her, and even though she never spoke back, I knew we'd become friends. Every now and again, I'd feel an arm around my shoulder. I wasn't scared, but felt really comfortable around her. It was sweet. I started calling her Caroline, and Caroline was invited to a lot of parties with the dolls and I."

Yet time went on, Davis' brother went away for school and Davis' social schedule suddenly got busier. She gradually stopped conversing with her ghostly friend as she grew older, and she noticed the girl's presence less and less. "One day my mother and I packed the dolls in my toy chest and put them up in the attic for good. I don't remember her being around too much after that," Davis says. "The house went quiet then. I thought about it every now and again—her leaving—and it made me sad."

Years passed, but Davis never forgot about the spirit that had stood up for her. Davis recalls: "I asked Ma about her a few times, but she couldn't tell me who the girl was. She said that she had been around just about as long as she could remember, and for all she knew had always had been around. Ma had never actually seen her either, but knew she was a girl because of how she loved dolls, and she had heard her whispering once or twice in her life. That was all we knew about her."

Both Davis and her brother inherited a desire to stay quiet about their household ghost. "My brother was a real story-teller, always regaling his friends with all sorts of tall tales," Davis says. "But in all his years, he never said anything about the girl who warned him to stay away from me." Neither did Davis herself.

"It was one of those things we never talked of," she says. "We all knew she was around. My whole family knew before me or my brother were even born, but everyone went on without thinking about it too much. I suppose ignoring Caroline was one of our family traditions. We accepted that she was there but never said a word. We never even asked who she was and why she was so attached to our home." Davis believes that she is the first to break this tradition of silence. And why?

"I said earlier that Caroline stopped showing up so much as I grew older. By the time I was a teenager, I barely noticed her at all." At the time, Davis occasionally wondered about the spirit's disappearing act, and she eventually came up with a halfhearted theory about how, after all those years, the ghost had gotten bored with haunting the Davis house. "I think there was a part of me that felt responsible," Davis says. "She had stayed around for my mother; why did she leave when I got older? There were a lot of times when I almost asked my mother about this, but like I said, Caroline was something that we barely ever discussed in our home. And I ended up not saying anything about it."

Davis would eventually get the answer to her question. "She never went anywhere. She'd been there all along. I think it was me that stopped seeing her."

After moving back to the family house years later, Davis found herself alone for the first time in her life. "My husband was gone and my children were all grown up. Nobody had been living in the house for a while, and I moved in thinking to spend some quiet years by myself." As it turned out, Davis would not be alone.

"I remember the first time I realized she was there. It was a few days after I was all settled in. I was in the kitchen having breakfast when I heard footsteps coming down the hall from the parlor. It was raining outside, and at first, I thought it was the wind or the rain." Then the footfalls entered the kitchen, and Davis was flooded with a warm, comforting and distantly familiar feeling. All at once, she knew her childhood friend was with her.

"I hadn't thought about Caroline in years and years," Davis says. "I thought she left us when I was a teenager, and that was it. That morning was wonderful. I felt like I was reunited with an old friend, and it was just so very nice. I said 'Hi Caroline,' out loud, and I felt her arm around my shoulder. It felt so small! I remember it being much bigger."

Since then, Davis says she has been enjoying her time with her ghostly little companion. "She still doesn't talk to me, but I can tell when she's there. I can hear her footsteps, and she's very affectionate. She likes to touch my shoulder, and sometimes my face. Sometimes, at night, I can hear her walking into my room and getting into bed with me. I know they say ghosts are supposed to be cold, but not Caroline. Her hands are always warm when she hugs me, and so is her side of the bed."

When her daughter's family visited, Davis had her son-in-law go up into the attic and bring her old toy chest down. "Bless 'em, the sweethearts looked a little bit worried when I asked for them to bring down my old toys. They probably thought I was losing my mind." Of course, Davis couldn't tell them the real reason she wanted her toy box.

"If I told them the dolls were for my invisible friend, Caroline, it's likely they would've locked me up," Davis laughs, "so I told them I wanted to sort and organize my old things, just to pass the time." That she did. As soon as her company left, Davis went about laying her dolls out in her old room as Caroline, who she knew was in the room, stood and watched.

"One of my favorite things to do is read up in my old bedroom. I know Caroline is there too because the dolls move off the dresser by themselves and have their own little party on the floor." An adult now, Davis doesn't sit down and play with Caroline the way she used to, though she still finds herself cleaning up after her friend, picking the dolls up off the floor and putting them back atop the dresser after Caroline is done. It is work she doesn't mind doing.

"I thought I would be spending a lot of time alone when I moved back here, but I feel so lucky to be living with my old friend. Caroline doesn't speak to me, and I still don't know what her real name is and why, of all places, she stays at my house. But I'm not too interested in the whos and the whys. I'm just happy to have her."

4
Spirits
of the Past

The Bells of Chartres Street

Once a year, every Good Friday just after midnight, it is said that the faint sound of bells can be heard coming from the small two-story building at 617 Chartres Street. Not everyone hears them when they ring, for there is nothing faint about the sounds of the French Quarter, and just down the street is Jackson Square, where the crowds, restaurants, musicians and street performers are often known to carry on well past midnight.

Still, they are audible to those who perhaps are paying a little more attention, and passersby have been known to stop suddenly, struck by a strange sound that seems simultaneously near and far, and by the inexplicable unease that grows with every ring. On some occasions the bells continue for several minutes; on others, they ring only a few times before falling silent. But the feeling is always the same. Whether they chime for seconds or minutes, there is always the same foreboding— the sense that the bells are warning of some approaching danger, some unforeseeable tragedy about to fall.

Not that anyone needs to panic when they chime. The bells on Chartres have been ringing for as long as anyone can remember, and to this day, no significant calamity has followed. Still, to those who've heard them, the feeling of foreboding has left a lasting impression, and more than a few have taken to looking for explanations. As anyone familiar with paranormal phenomena knows, ready causes are almost always found in the past. Study the history of a haunted place, and you are likely to come across an explanation for its ghosts. In the case of the bells of Chartres, the history points to one single incident—not a pending catastrophe, but one that transpired years ago, just after midnight on a windy Good Friday, March 21, 1788.

Don Vincente Nunez, Treasurer of Louisiana, was up late, saying prayers in front of his personal altar. Did he notice that the window beside the altar was open, and that the drapes were blowing a bit too close to the candles on the altar? If he did, the treasurer did nothing about it.

Like most of the buildings in New Orleans at the time, Nunez's house was made of cypress wood, and after his curtains caught fire, it was just a matter of minutes before the rest of his house was ablaze. In a panic, Nunez went running out of his house and down the street to the little church of St. Louis, where he hollered to the priests that the fire was spreading through his home, and he insisted that they ring the church bells to warn the community.

If Nunez had shown up minutes earlier, the priests would've gladly sounded the alarm, summoning every able-bodied resident to put out the blaze. But it was just past midnight, and the church didn't allow the bells to be rung on Good Friday. Critical moments passed as Nunez continued to plead with the priest. Only when the glow from the burning house became visible from the church did the cleric finally concede. By then, it was too late.

The bells had been tied and covered so that they wouldn't ring accidentally, and as the two men struggled to untie them, the fire was spreading from the treasurer's home. Fanned by the strong winds, the blaze spread with devastating swiftness, destroying half of the Vieux Carre in a matter of hours. When the destruction had finally run its course the next morning, over 800 homes had burned to the ground, along with the town hall, the church and the rectory on the

The bells of 617 Chartres Street can still be heard, if one listens very carefully.

Place d'Arms. It isn't known for certain how many lost their lives that night, but Governor Esteban Miro's report speaks volumes. After surveying the ruin, he wrote of the now-destitute families whose faces "told the ruin of a city which in less than five hours has been transformed into an arid and horrible wilderness."

Could such mass destruction have been prevented if the priest had rung the church bells as soon as Vincente Nunez approached him? Or if the bells hadn't been tied down? Maybe if the city had been warned just a few minutes earlier, the damage would not have been so bad. And there's also the matter of Don Vincente's altar. If only he had been paying attention to the curtain and the candle flames, or if he had been quicker in snuffing out the fire before it spread through his house. Could Nunez have guessed, as he ran out of his house and down Chartres Street to the St. Louis Catherdral, that his home was to become the epicenter of New Orleans' worst disaster to date?

While the gravity of the situation may well have been clear, there's no way Nunez would have guessed, or even considered, the far-reaching consequences of that night's events. Though his house was destroyed by fire that night, every building that has since stood in its place has also been haunted by the tragedy of New Orleans' first great fire. Today, at the humble building on 617 Chartres Street, the bells that ought to have rang that fateful Good Friday can be heard once a year, chiming faintly over the span of centuries—almost inaudible and far, far too late.

Little Napoleon

Pierre Gustave Toutant Beauregard was one of the premier generals of the Confederate Army. A native Louisianan who showed great promise in West Point, graduating second in his class, he rose to military prominence during the Mexican War and was appointed superintendent of West Point just months before the Civil War broke out. Beauregard was a stern and competent officer whose pride in his Southern roots equaled his military reputation, so no one was surprised when he made the decision to pitch in with the Confederate cause.

It was General Beauregard who was responsible for the opening shots of the Civil War, ordering the bombardment of Fort Sumter on April 13, 1861. The Southern papers made the acclaimed "Hero of Fort Sumter" into something of a celebrity, and a few short months later, he commanded the Confederate Army of the Potomac to victory during the first Battle of Bull Run. Dubbed "Little Napoleon" by his military peers for his admiration of Napoleon Bonaparte, after Bull Run the Creole general might have dared to dream of a legacy comparable to that of his martial idol. If he did entertain any such fantasies of military glory, they were quashed in early April 1862, when Beauregard took command of the Confederate forces during the Battle of Shiloh.

The first major engagement in the Civil War's western theater, Shiloh saw the meeting of 65,000 Union soldiers with roughly 44,000 Confederates on the west bank of the Tennessee River over April 6 and 7. It was a bloody, two-day seesaw of attack and counterattack, and when the smoke cleared over the contested ground, there were over 24,000 dead, wounded and missing, with the Union forces standing victorious over the field. Beauregard's first loss was a major blow to the Confederacy. The Union victory at Shiloh led to the occupation of Corinth, Mississippi, a major railway hub for the Confederacy and a key strategic location.

By all accounts, General Beauregard had difficulty dealing with what he experienced at Shiloh. Shortly after retreating from Corinth, "Little Napoleon" went on a sick leave for over two months without Jefferson Davis' permission. The Confederate president was outraged at the general's insubordination, and he ordered that Beauregard be permanently stripped of his military rank. By September of that year, a shortage of skilled officers saw Davis rescinding his order, and Beauregard was reinstated to a military command. Beauregard served the Confederate Army for the duration of the Civil War, but he would never live up to the promise of his first months.

Resigned to civilian life after the Confederate defeat, Beauregard went on to become one of New Orleans' leading citizens, making a tidy sum in railroad development and serving a term as Louisiana's adjutant general. But despite his post-war affluence, Beauregard seems to have had some difficulty leaving the war behind him—especially the Battle of Shiloh. Indeed, the strange and inexplicable experiences of many who have visited the Beauregard-Keyes House in New Orleans' French Quarter have led many to believe that what the general saw at the critical Tennessee battle left a deep and lasting mark on the psyche of New Orleans' "Little Napoleon." Beauregard lived in the house that bears his name for only one year, calling the stately old mansion home from 1865 to 1866. A short time, yes, but apparently

General Beauregard was dubbed "Little Napoleon" by his military peers.

a time in his life that he would never forget, a time that was loaded with tortured memories of the first battle he lost.

Stories about the Beauregard-Keyes House first emerged in 1893, the same year the general passed away. It was in that year that people walking by Beauregard's former residence late at night first heard the voice. The voice was old and raspy, and it spoke one word over and over in a tone that landed somewhere between horror and regret. "Shiloh... Shiloh," it groaned.

None who heard the mournful mantra believed it came from anyone, or anything, that lived. It was distinctly unnatural, a voice barely above a whisper that somehow seemed to come from a very great distance. It was as if a man somewhere inside the darkened house was lost in a nightmare, muttering the object of his dread over and over in a fitful sleep. And yet passersby were able to hear the terrified whispers as if the sleeping man was lying right next to them, conveying his terror on all who heard the two tortured syllables. Many who heard the name of the Civil War battle found themselves running away from the Beauregard-Keyes House as fast as their legs could carry them.

It didn't take long for people to link the whispering voice to the house's former resident who lost the battle with the same name as the whispered word. The assumption that some post-mortem remnant of General Beauregard still resided in the New Orleans mansion gained currency when house residents began to talk of a semi-transparent apparition that manifested in the ballroom in the middle of the night. According to witnesses, the shimmering figure was dressed in a Confederate's gray military uniform and bore a striking resemblance to photographs of Beauregard as he appeared in the prime of his life. Most people who saw the general standing in the ballroom did not stand around gaping for long. The sight of Beauregard was often accompanied by a severe temperature drop that chilled witnesses to the bone. Some who saw the general claimed that they were moved by an almost instinctual drive to turn around and run, sensing that the figure standing in front of them was a ghostly expression of pure misery.

Luckily for those living in the Beauregard-Keyes House, the ghost of General Beauregard did not stay in the ballroom for long. It is not known exactly when he stopped appearing, but within one year, reports of run-ins with Beauregard's ghost stopped. Yet whatever relief residents of the mansion may have felt was short-lived; soon after Beauregard's spirit ceased its loitering in the ballroom, another equally disturbing phenomenon began to occur. The general and his solitary cry for the battle he lost was replaced by a supernatural manifestation of the battle itself—the ballroom transformed before startled witnesses' eyes into a ghostly Shiloh, complete with bugles, drums, rifles, artillery and casualties.

The sounds of the battle were heard only late in the evening, and like Beauregard's whisper, were tinged with surreal intonation, somehow sounding very far and very near at the same time. Anyone awakened late at night could follow the ruckus down to the ballroom, where, according to legend, they were in for quite a sight.

There, instead of the Beauregard-Keyes ballroom, was a sort of phantom rendition of the Battle of Shiloh. Those who witnessed it told of rows of weary-looking men standing in a surreal landscape dotted by vague visions of trees, rivers and hills. Some likened the sight to an impressionist painting,

The Battle of Shiloh continues to be fought within the Beauregard-Keyes House.

others to some bizarre dreamscape they were more likely to see in their sleep. The men standing in their stolid rows—soldiers from the North and the South—did not actually fight but remained deathly still, staring ahead expressionless as the muted sound of battle boomed and cracked through the erstwhile ballroom. Long moments would pass during which most witnesses, awestruck or frightened, believed that they were looking upon some sort of supernatural roll call—until they realized that, one by one, the soldiers in front of them were taking injuries. It happened with every crash of cannon and fusillade of rifle fire: one member of the phantom troop would suddenly be perforated through the chest, another would lose an arm, yet another would have his leg blown off and crumple to the ground. And still they remained there, the dead of Shiloh, staring ahead in silence even as they were being cut down by the distant sounds of rifle and cannon.

Many witnesses to the haunting in the ballroom turn and run before the ghostly battle has run its course, but those possessed more by curiosity than by fear stand and watch until each soldier is struck down. Then a speedy decomposition begins: the visage of every fallen soldier rapidly changes into a grinning skull, and the cuts and lacerations of wounded limbs fade into clean bone. Then they are gone. The supernatural scene always ends the same way, concluding the moment the morning sun rises over New Orleans. The mass of skeletal apparitions gradually fades into nothingness, and the furnishings of the Beauregard-Keyes ballroom gradually replace the hills and trees of the ghostly Shiloh. By the time the sun has risen, not a trace of the supernatural battle remains.

Unlike the ghost of General Beauregard, the phantom battle has continued to be reported throughout the years. Subsequent owners spoke of the strange sights and sounds in the ballroom, and reports of the phenomenon continued throughout the 20th century, even after the doors of the Beauregard-Keyes House were opened to the public when the mansion was made into a National Historic Site. Passersby late at night still talk about sounds of battle coming from within. And despite statements by the house's caretakers that they have never seen anything out of the ordinary in the ballroom, the house curators have acknowledged that something about the house frightens them. A good number of paranormal enthusiasts and investigators alike consider the house to be one of New Orleans' premier haunted sites.

It is interesting that the ghost of General Beauregard stopped appearing after so short a time, while the ghostly vision of Shiloh, his greatest defeat, continues to be reported today, over 100 years later. Could this be evidence of how deeply the Louisianan general was affected by what he experienced on the Tennessee battlefield? Perhaps Beauregard was a more sensitive man than history gives him credit for—a man who suffered greatly for the horror he saw on April 6 and April 7, 1862. He lived in the Beauregard-Keyes House for only one year after the Civil War, but perhaps the memory of the battle was so intense that he could not let himself forget it. Could he have wandered down to the ballroom during sleepless nights and relived—in the same feverish delirium experienced by so many other veterans who lived through horrific battles—night after night, the details of those two terrible days? Were these flashbacks so intense that they left some sort of psychic residue in the ballroom that is still felt today? This would mean that the haunting in the Beauregard-Keyes House is not the ghosts of the soldiers who died at Shiloh, but the ghosts of General Beauregard's nightmares—the remnants of one man's struggles with the horrors of the Civil War.

The Curve in the Tracks

Why they are heard on some evenings and not others is a mystery. On most nights, nothing out of the ordinary occurs on the Kansas City Southern Railroad line that runs through Bossier Parish. A locomotive may rumble by; perhaps there's the distant booming of cars locking and re-aligning. Nothing out of the ordinary.

But there are other nights when terrifying and piteous screams echo up and down a bend in the tracks. They are always heard around the same time—between 10:30 and 11:30 at night—and around the same place, at one curve on the KCS line in Bossier City. A shrill and horrifying chorus of screams has a way of sticking with the railway men who have heard it.

It is believed they are the dying screams of a young family. The legend tells us that a woman and her children perished on the track years ago, when their vehicle stalled before an oncoming train. Ever since, the bend where the mother and children met their end has acquired a cursed reputation—drawing the interest of local paranormal enthusiasts and spooking the railway men who have to work there.

Père Dagobert and the Phantom Funeral Procession

At night, some might say that it looks like an apparition itself. St. Louis Cathedral rises from the end of Jackson Square, its smooth brickwork lit an ethereal white, its three black spires rising into the blackness of the New Orleans night.

Most evenings, the square beneath these spires is littered with candlelit tables, where self-proclaimed oracles, fortune-tellers and palm and tarot readers offer to give tourists a glimpse of the future. There are musicians competing with the bustle from the restaurants and the shouts of revelers spilling off Bourbon Street. In the wake of all this, the cathedral stands in the background, silent and still, almost incidental to the hammering pulse of the French Quarter.

And yet there are other nights—nights when the wind carries something unsettling through the Vieux Carré's cramped streets. Nights when the black water of the Mississippi whispers something of the past as it crawls by, the same something that the rain seems to want to say as it falls over Jackson Square. Those who happen to be in the square on such nights can't help but notice the way the St. Louis looks, glowing moon-like with disquieting intensity, somehow bigger than usual, somehow *alive*. Then, from somewhere inside, an eerie melody emerges. A sorrowful song in another language grows louder and louder. It seems to be emanating from inside the cathedral, but the door is still shut and there is no one there. The words are audible now: "Kyrie eleison, kyrie eleison," sung over and over in mournful elegy—the Catholic supplication for mercy on the souls of the dead.

The song continues to grow louder, more distinct, until it is clearly heard over the wind and the rain. No longer confined to the cathedral, it seems to be everywhere, ringing off the buildings and streets, faint yet clear, distant yet also very near. Just when it seems as if the song is about to become real, however—at the moment it seems to be clear and tangible enough to belong to a human voice—it begins to fade. Slowly back into obscurity it fades, drowned out by the wind and the rain, until it is silenced completely, leaving stunned witnesses standing in wonder, gazing up at the shining cathedral from where it came.

This Jackson Square kyrie is among the city's oldest legends, almost as ancient as the cathedral itself. The story finds its roots in the early 1760s when Louisiana was still French territory and the 13 colonies had yet to become the United States. The French-Indian War was raging over the continent, with French and English armies clashing on northeastern battlefields, while guerilla warfare along the frontier pitted settlers against Indians in countless merciless skirmishes.

By 1762, the French knew it was only a matter of time. Their small colony in the north was dwarfed by the British settlements along the Atlantic. Fully aware that they were poised to lose the war and their possessions to the English, they drafted the Treaty of Fontainebleau, ceding all their holdings west of the Mississippi, including what was then called the Isle of New Orleans, to the Spanish. So began the era of Spanish rule over the Louisiana Territory, which lasted from 1762 until the French took it back in 1800.

As dramatic as the imperial powers' diplomatic maneuverings were, they were conducted independently of the people who lived in the colonies in question. In 1762, there

Jackson Square in front of St. Louis Cathedral

wasn't a man or woman in New Orleans who knew that they had passed from French to Spanish rule. Indeed, it wasn't until 1766, when the Spanish sent its first governor, Don Antonio de Ulloa, that the colonists on the Mississippi Delta discovered the French crown had traded them away.

They didn't take it well. The French colonists weren't willing to accept a Spanish rule, and after two years of festering anger, they launched what would be the continent's first colonial revolt against a European power. Frightened by rumors that the Spanish were going to sell them into slavery, the French cast out the Spanish authority, sending Don Antonio and his retinue fleeing for Cuba.

The second governor sent by the Spanish, an Irish mercenary named Alejandro O'Reilly, arrived in August of 1769. Landing in New Orleans at the head of 24 ships and over 2000 soldiers, O'Reilly came ready for a fight, and the fiery Irishman's willingness to resort to brutal force soon earned him the moniker "Bloody O'Reilly." Charged by the Spanish crown to root out the French insurgents, one of the new governor's first actions was to arrest leading men in the community suspected of being ringleaders of the rebellion. O'Reilly issued a pardon to the general population, then turned around and clapped the irons on the 10 men he believed had led the insurgence. Three months later, in October of that year, O'Reilly passed his judgment.

Charged with treason, sedition, writing inflammatory documents and leading men against the authority of the Spanish crown, three of the men were banished from Louisiana for life, one was handed a life sentence in a Cuban prison, five were sentenced to death by firing squad and the last was stabbed to death while in captivity. Though such sentencing, harsh by today's standards, could not have been such a shock to the colonists, it was the decree that followed that earned O'Reilly his reputation for cruelty.

According to legend, O'Reilly ordered that the six executed men be denied a proper burial. Instead, their bodies were to be left to the mercy of the elements, laid out in plain sight on Jackson Square, their rotting corpses a grotesque reminder of treason's ultimate end. The colonists were a religious people;

in their eyes, execution for treason was one thing, but to deny Christian men the right of a consecrated burial was the worst kind of maliciousness.

The victims' families pleaded with the governor to reconsider, but O'Reilly held fast, determined to set an example. There would be no clemency for treason. Under constant watch of a Spanish guard, the bodies were left to decompose in plain sight. That is, until Père Dagobert took it upon himself to intercede.

New Orleans' most beloved pastor, Père Dagobert was a Capuchin monk who had been pastor of the St. Louis Cathedral since 1745. A natural leader among his people, Dagobert had spent nearly 30 years administering to the spiritual needs of the colony. During a time when life was nasty, brutish and short, Père Dagobert stood for mercy and compassion, caring for the sick and poor, providing comfort to the bereaved. He dedicated himself selflessly to his flock, and they reciprocated his love with the truest admiration. An ardent Catholic and dedicated humanist, he was not able to stand by and watch the Spanish governor desecrate the bodies of his parishioners.

On a stormy night shortly after the executions, Dagobert visited the families of the dead, going to one mourning house after another, instructing them to follow him back to the church. When they were all assembled there, he ushered them into a small room and told them to wait, promising that he would return shortly. Locking the door behind him, Dagobert went out into the rainy night, where he remained until the small hours of the morning.

The monk let the families out when he had completed his task, leading them into the church's main chamber by

St. Louis Cemetery No. 1

candlelight. There, lying in front of the altar, draped in black cloth, were the bodies of the six executed men. To this day, how Dagobert managed to circumvent the guards and get the bodies into the church remains a mystery, but he did it for the families and, perhaps, in obligation to his own sense of responsibility. There was no way such a dedicated pastor could allow six of his flock to go without proper burial. Christian men denied their last rights? O'Reilly's edict was a personal affront to Père Dagobert's station.

And so the priest defied Bloody O'Reilly, providing the six men with a proper burial. The funeral began in the church, where Dagobert sang his mournful kyrie. Into the rainy night he and the six mourning families marched, carrying the bodies of the dead on their shoulders. The nocturnal procession made its way through the streets, with Père Dagobert singing all the way to St. Louis Cemetery No. 1, where the bodies were entombed in anonymous graves.

The people of New Orleans would never forget Père Dagobert for this act. Risking the wrath of a brutal governor, the priest went ahead and gave six of the colony's leading men a proper burial. He died in 1776 and, like other famous New Orleans prelates, was interred in a crypt under the church altar.

Folklore would have us believe that the spirit of the priest never truly departed, that it is indeed his voice heard on Jackson Square in the small hours of certain evenings. On such nights, when the rain falls hard and there's a slight chill in the air, Dagobert's clear voice is heard at the head of the phantom funeral procession—heard, but not seen, still singing a kyrie for the souls of the six men who were killed standing against Spanish rule.

The Taylortown Tower

Off US Highway 71, south of Bossier City, lies an unusual sight. There, standing alone in a verdurous pasture, is a church bell tower without a church. An orange brick construction with long gothic arches, the tower is all that is left of the old Methodist Church of Taylortown. It could be the way the wind whistles through the Gothic arches or just how the solitary ruin looks as it rises over the landscape of the northwest corner of Louisiana, that makes one think that there *ought* to be a ghost haunting the Taylortown Tower.

Indeed, there was said to be a ghost in the bell tower even before the church burned down in the 1940s. The legend finds its roots sometime in the early 1900s, on the day that two young lovers had planned to be married. The tale begins outside the Taylortown church with an anxious bride surrounded by her equally anxious bridesmaids. At that moment, she was supposed to be arm in arm with her father, marching down the aisle to her waiting fiancé. But that wasn't happening. Rather, she was the one who was waiting, along with her father, the bridesmaids, the guests and the pastor, for a groom who was nowhere to be found.

She had begun to fear what she thought was the worst—that he had gotten cold feet and run out on her—when one of her fiancé's groomsmen arrived at the church, covered in blood, with news far worse than her worst fear. There had been a car accident. Her fiancé was dead.

Different versions of the story emerge here. One has her running to the top of the bell tower in a fit of disbelief, desperately hoping to get a glimpse of her approaching fiancé. She stayed up there for hours, her anxious hope gradually turning to delirious grief. She was still in a state of shock when her friends convinced her to come back down. While descending, she stumbled and fell, cracking her skull on her way down. The bride lay dead at the foot of the stairs. Another version has her surviving her would-be wedding day, but going mad from grief. Somehow, she convinced herself that her fiancé was still trying to get to the church, and she insisted on waiting for him at the top of the bell tower. Sustained by a hopeful delirium, she waited there for days and days. When her bubble finally burst, she was overcome by despondency. They found her the next day, a noose around her neck, hanging from the rafters of the bell tower.

Whatever version of her demise one subscribes to, the bell tower was said to be haunted after she died. On certain evenings, at the stroke of midnight, she can be heard screaming from the top of the tower as the bell tolls. This was said to continue even after the church burned down and the tower was abandoned—said to continue, indeed, to this very day.

The Ghost of Père Antoine and the St. Louis Cathedral

Père Dagobert was nearing the end of his life around 1774, when Friar Antonio de Sedella arrived in New Orleans with the Spanish Inquisition. Legend has it that he had been sent to Louisiana to institute the inquisition in the colony, but once he had gotten to know New Orleans, he was unwilling to bring the brutal investigation down on the community. This was only the first of many actions that would endear the monk, who would become known as Père Antoine, to his new parishioners.

Over the years, Père Antoine baptized practically every child born in New Orleans and presided over most of the weddings. A parish could hardly have asked for a more active priest. He worked endlessly for the well-being of the city's slave population while tending to the needs of the free men, women and children of color. Père Antoine dedicated himself entirely to the Spanish colony on the Mississippi Delta.

When the St. Louis Cathedral burned down in 1788, Père Antoine was appointed pastor of the cathedral that went up in its place, and he kept his station over the newly designated cathedral until his death in 1829. Like Père Dagobert before him, Antoine was entombed under St. Louis' altar. However, his story does not end there.

The stories started with parishioners who claimed to see the late priest during Christmas Eve Midnight Mass. Even today, there is always at least one person among the congregation who will gasp at the sight of a man walking along the left side of the altar. He is always the same, dressed in his

Capuchin robes, carrying a candle, walking away from the altar toward the praying congregation, gradually fading out of sight with every step he takes, until he vanishes completely. No one knows why he chooses to appear at this time, on this day, or why he's visible to some people and not others, but the Christmas sightings have been reported for longer than anyone can remember. The first took place the first Midnight Mass after the beloved priest died.

Père Antoine's spirit is not confined to the church alone. His likeness has also been spotted in the early morning, walking down the small alley that bears his name along the side of the cathedral. He always appears in his black robes, his nose buried in a breviary as he goes. Those who claim to have seen the robed figure in Père Antoine's Alley invariably bring up the sensation of good will that wells up within them as he passes, and the great calm that washes over them as he walks by. But he never remains for long, always vanishing from sight before he reaches the end of the alley.

There is one account of a woman walking down the alley by herself in the afternoon. Supposedly, this woman was walking a bit too briskly for the high heels she had on, and she lost her balance and tumbled over. Luckily, a man appeared out of nowhere, catching her before she hit the ground. When she straightened up, she found herself staring at a sharp-nosed man dressed in black robes. A severe expression etched onto his stony face, he appraised her sternly, his eyes looking straight through her. The woman glanced down for an instant to brush off her skirt; when she looked up again, there was no trace of the man who had caught her just a moment ago. Right then, she heard a voice whispering. The voice was audible enough for her to know

Père Antoine's spirit has been seen walking down this small alley along the side of the cathedral.

that it was a man's, and that it was French, but she wasn't able to make out what this voice was saying. Regardless, as soon as the voice spoke, she was overcome with a sudden feeling of peace.

The Pirate Jean Lafitte

It is fitting, given New Orleans' penchant for meshing myth with history and magic with the mundane, that there is almost no reliable information on one of the city's most celebrated figures. Jean Lafitte—year of birth unknown, year of death likewise—was a handsome, swashbuckling pirate whose 100-ship fleet sailed the Gulf of Mexico, stealing from the rich and giving to the poor. Or that's what some say. Others maintain that there was nothing at all heroic about the legendary figure—that he was a short, unimposing man with a love of money and a double chin. The only thing this version of the legendary pirate has in common with his more dashing incarnation is that Lafitte got rich off high-seas robbery. Yet unlike the handsome swashbuckler, this Lafitte never once clutched a saber in his hand or robbed a ship personally. Rather, he gave the order to do so to one of his many subordinates.

Chances are, if Lafitte himself were alive today, he would be just fine with his questionable place in the annals of the city's history. In fact, while he was alive, he did everything he could to foster an air of mystery. Depending on who wanted to know, Lafitte was either born in Marseille, Bordeaux or St. Dominigue. If he was speaking to some Southern belle he believed to be afflicted with a romantic disposition, he would say he was a French nobleman who had just barely escaped the Revolution's guillotines. On other occasions, he claimed to have fled to New Orleans in the wake of the Haiti slave revolt. The truth? Thanks to Lafitte's imagination, and his desire to be all things to all people, no one will ever know.

Not that everything about the man is a mystery. There are some things that are known. Most histories are consistent with the date of his first appearance in New Orleans—1803. Also, he wasn't exactly a pirate, but a privateer. Thus, he didn't rob every ship he came across, but only Spanish vessels, which was justified because he was sailing with letters of marque from Cartagena, a Spanish colony that was fighting the Crown for its independence. It's generally accepted that he was incredibly proficient at relieving Spanish ships of their valuables—so much so that his contemporaries began heaping monikers upon him like medals on a war hero. He was "The Corsair," "The Buccaneer," "The Terror of the Gulf," "The King of Barataria" and "The Hero of New Orleans." It is these last two sobriquets that figure largest in the history of a certain bar on Bourbon Street that the mercurial pirate's ghost is said to haunt.

Jean Lafitte's base of operations was in Barataria Bay, a swampy body of water cutting into the Delta, just south of New Orleans. With a pirate fleet of roughly 100 ships and over 1000 men, Lafitte boasted complete control of the bay. It was here that the lucre of his raids was accumulated and then sent out to be sold on the New Orleans black market. These black markets may have been where Lafitte earned his reputation as "The Creole Robin Hood," for any item purchased from his pirate merchants, be they fine linens, silverware, jewelry, spices or furniture, were substantially cheaper than the same items subjected to tariffs and sold legally.

His alias of "The Hero of New Orleans" was not given without irony, as there were definitely times when Lafitte was at odds with the authorities in the city. It began soon after 1803, when Jefferson made his historic purchase of

New Orleans and the sprawling Louisiana Territory from Napoleon. When the authorities began arriving from Washington, they found that the culture of their newly acquired city was very different from what they knew among the settlements along the Atlantic. Most of the locals spoke French. They were Catholic. And many had a far more easy-going approach to life, liberty and the pursuit of happiness. But what really bothered William Claiborne, the territory's first American governor, was the local Creoles' lax attitude towards smuggled goods. Every tax-free gilded teaspoon that Lafitte sold in his illegal markets was money the government lost.

Yet as much as the Claiborne government despised smuggling, there wasn't much that could be done about it. In many ways, the Americans were foreigners in this nearly one-century-old colony. And as much as they looked down on the Creole population, which they perceived as indolent and lawless, so too did the locals dislike their new masters, thinking them boorish and uncultured. In 1813, when Claiborne tried to stop Lafitte's smuggling by putting a $500 price on the pirate's head, Lafitte responded by issuing a bounty of his own. Standing before a cheering crowd outside his blacksmith's shop on Bourbon Street, the pirate announced that he would give $1500 to any man who brought him Claiborne's head.

How then, did such a zealous outlaw become "The Hero of New Orleans"? Two words: the British. When the War of 1812 broke out, the British approached Lafitte's base in Barataria, offering him gold, land title and a commission in the Royal Navy if he helped them infiltrate the bayous of southern Louisiana. Lafitte sent the British envoy off, promising that he would consider the offer. What he did instead, however, was immediately send Claiborne a letter informing him of the British plan. For as much as Lafitte clashed with the governor and the American authority, he had a certain respect for the American constitution and the ideals it represented. As zealously as he broke the law, never once did he attack a ship flying the United States flag. And when it came down to a decision between the English and the Americans, he chose those he loved to antagonize so much.

While Claiborne took note of the Lafitte's warning, he had no intention of allying with his nemesis and rejected Lafitte's offer of aid. It's a good thing for the Americans that Lafitte didn't take it personally. Ignoring Claiborne, Lafitte approached Andrew Jackson, the Tennesse soldier who had come south to defend New Orleans from the British. At first, Jackson also turned down the aid of Lafitte and the "hellish banditti" he led. But the future president changed his mind under the weight of the impending British advance. Unable to say no to the 1000 Batarian men and 7500 flints with powder Lafitte offered, Jackson finally capitulated to necessity and took a pirate into his ranks. By all reports, Lafitte and his 1000-man contingent fought heroically during the Battle of New Orleans.

Willing as he was to stand for the United States, Lafitte's contribution to the country's defense would not be appreciated for long. Though Lafitte was officially pardoned of his piracy after the Battle of New Orleans, within a few years, he found himself once more on the wrong side of the law. He may have received a presidential pardon but all the property he had illegally amassed received no such protection, and he was forced to leave Barataria after Claiborne had the pirate's

The Battle of New Orleans

loot confiscated and his ships seized. In 1821, the United States Navy informed him that if he and his men did not abandon their new colony on Galveston Island, they would be forcibly removed. Nursing a bitter grudge that would last the rest of his life, Lafitte left Galveston and vanished from the history books.

Everything written of Lafitte after this point is pure supposition. The more romantic narratives have him dying as he lived—falling in battle while fighting off a fleet of pirates in the Caribbean. Another theory tells of a less valiant demise— overcome by yellow fever, breathing his last on a sickbed on the Yucatan Peninsula. Still more optimistic renditions of his life take a bizarre twist, finding the once-dreaded pirate in Illinois with a family and a homestead, dying peacefully in his bedroom, an old man surrounded by family. And of course, there's the theory that he actually never left New Orleans, the city that he loved so much. Indeed, that some people say his spirit still resides there to this day.

Jean Lafitte's Blacksmith Shop bills itself as one of the oldest bars in the United States. It certainly looks it. An ancient two-story shop constructed with building techniques used by the earliest French settlers, the establishment is one of the few buildings in the French Quarter that survived both of New Orleans' great fires of the 18th century. The old blacksmith shop stands apart from the Spanish-influenced architecture that dominates the Vieux Carre. Without the second floor galleries or intricate ironwork that mark its neighbors, the bar is obviously from another era. Its plaster is crumbling, and exposed timbers cut through orange brick.

Today, Jean Lafitte's Blacksmith Shop largely owes its fame to two facts: one, that it is one of the few establishments in the French Quarter dating past Spanish rule; and two, that it is said to be haunted by the spirit of the famous pirate. Though not everyone agrees , according to some versions of the city's history, Lafitte once used the building as an undercover depot, where he stored all the booty he smuggled into the city. Even then, the story goes, the establishment was known as Jean Lafitte's Blacksmith Shop, just a thin front for what was *really* going on within those walls. But it was more than an illegal warehouse. It was also Jean Lafitte's favorite place in town. Indeed, it was said that if "The Terror of the Gulf" was in New Orleans, odds were he could be found at the smithy, either taking inventory of his ill-gotten gains, or sharing drinks around a gambling table with his most trusted partners. Given the drinking exploits Lafitte and men of his ilk were famous for, one can only imagine all the nights of raucous revelry that passed there.

Some things never change. For while stolen treasure can no longer be found within those walls, there is still raucous revelry to be had, if patrons desire it. One of the French Quarter's most popular bars, Jean Lafitte's Blacksmith Shop definitely cashes in on its rich history and the ghost of a famous man who evidently still has a bit of carousing left in him.

Charlene Lavallee would vouch for it. "My husband and I went to New Orleans three years ago for our honeymoon," she begins. "We both wanted to see it, and we waited four months after the wedding to go, when the weather was nice. We didn't go there because of the voodoo or the ghosts or the vampires, even though now I know this is why many people go to the French Quarter."

Lavallee goes on to say that once they got there, however, they ended up going on a walking tour through some of the haunted sites of the French Quarter. "We saw the tours first in the brochures, and at night when we went out they were all over the place. It was funny to us because we didn't think about ghosts when we went, but the tours were everywhere. At first we wondered about it. My husband especially was curious. So we said, 'Why not?'"

She didn't regret it. "There are a lot of things that happened in New Orleans. Much history. It was funny to learn about it like this—with all the crazy stories about the murders and the fires and the ghosts. I don't think my husband or I believed in it too much. Or maybe we did just a little bit. You never know, right? Anything can happen."

Jean Lafitte's Blacksmith Shop

Skeptical but open-minded, Lavallee was in for quite a shock that night. "On this tour we walked through the street until the guide stopped at a place he said had ghosts inside. He would tell us a story about the house from the street, and then we kept walking. We never went inside any of the houses, and the whole time my husband and I didn't see anything." Though neither she nor her husband witnessed any of the spirits their guide was telling them about, Lavallee enjoyed herself, and after the tour was over, she was in the mood for more walking.

"When we were in the street called Pirate's Alley, our guide talked about Jean Lafitte," Lavallee says, "but we never went to the Blacksmith Shop. He didn't say anything about a ghost there. It's funny."

Funny. They might have walked right by the Blacksmith Shop if it wasn't for the laughter spilling out onto the street. "As soon as I saw it, I wanted to go in," Lavallee says. "It was dark on the street, and inside it was dark too. There was no electricity, only candles, and the bar was very, very old. Maybe the oldest building we saw since we were there. It looked very romantic, and I almost dragged my husband inside."

The Blacksmith Shop was crowded when the pair walked in, as it is on most nights, and Lavallee's love for the place grew once they were inside. "Inside was gorgeous," Lavallee continues. "We had to almost squeeze in to walk, but it was so nice. There was a man playing a small piano in the back. Right away, it was my favorite bar in the city."

They were lucky that a group was leaving just as they were arriving, and the couple grabbed the table. The drinks started coming after that. "We were having a wonderful time. It was a good day, and we were talking about everything we saw. You couldn't see across the bar because it was so dark and crowded inside, but it was so special. It's hard to explain, but it was so *real* inside, you know? We could have been sitting down there 200 years ago, and I think it would have looked very much the same."

Caught up in the moment with her husband, Lavallee didn't say anything the first time she felt the chill creep over her. "All the doors to the bars were open," she says, "but it was a very nice night, with no wind. So I thought it was strange that I felt cold. But the first time it came and it went very quickly, and I didn't think about it too much." That was the first time.

"I don't know, maybe it was a few minutes later, when I had the feeling of cold again," Lavallee continues. "This time, it was worse. It wasn't like a normal cold from cold weather. It was more as though the cold was coming from *inside*. I felt it like a cold hand in my back. It came so fast it made me jump in my seat."

Lavallee's husband noticed his wife's sudden discomfort and asked her if there was anything wrong. "I asked him about the cold, but he didn't feel anything. He got a little concerned and asked if I wanted to go." Lavallee says she didn't even consider it. Thinking it would be a shame to end such a perfect night because of a chill, Lavallee told herself all she needed was to get up for a moment. She rose to go to the restroom, telling her husband that she would be right back.

"The feeling didn't go away when I was going to the restroom, though," she says. "It even got worse. Even though everybody else was fine, talking and laughing, for me it was very strange. I started to have a feeling when I was going to the restroom that somebody was following me." She turned to look, but there was nobody there. Rushing now, she made her way forward. Then—relief. As soon as she stepped into the restroom, the inexplicable cold subsided somewhat. She splashed water on her face and got ready to walk back out into the bar, assuming that the worst was over.

"The cold came again when I was back in the bar, and that was when I knew for sure that something weird was happening there." Lavallee laughs. "I thought about the ghost tour when I was going back to the table. My husband and I were walking around for over one hour listening to a man talk about dead people and ghosts. Could be that I was imagining something?" She laughs again. "Then I thought that maybe there was a ghost following me around. You know, this Jean Lafitte's Blacksmith Shop was a very old building, after all."

As preposterous as the thought seemed at the time, Lavallee's attitude toward the supernatural was about to take as sharp turn toward credulity. "I saw him when I sat down," she says. " I was going to tell my husband what was happening and then he was there, only a few feet away. He was standing right in the middle of three people who were talking, but they didn't notice him. Nobody could see him."

She was certain because if everybody else could've seen him, he would have been the center of attention. "It was dark, but from what I could see, he was a very handsome man," Lavallee continues. "He had broad shoulders. It was hard to see his face very clearly, but I could see that he had a very big mustache, and also a big hat that I've never seen anybody wear before.

"It was funny to me because when I saw him, all at once the cold I was feeling was gone. I felt normal again, and also calm. Even though I couldn't see his face too clearly in the dark, I knew this man was smiling at me." Lavallee smiled back in spite of herself, causing her husband to look over his shoulder. Seeing nothing out of the ordinary in the darkened room, he turned back and asked his wife what she was smiling at. "I looked away from the man for maybe two or three seconds to say to my husband, 'Can't you see that man?' But when I looked back, he was gone.

"We went on a history tour later that week," she said, "and on this one, our guide took us by the Blacksmith Shop. That was when I learned the story about the pirate, Jean Lafitte. When our guide was finished talking about the bar, she joked that some people say they see the ghost of Lafitte when they go there at night. Everyone laughed except for me and my husband." Now convinced that she saw the ghost of the legendary pirate, Lavallee goes on to say that she developed an enduring fascination with pirate lore after her honeymoon, and read everything on the topic she could get her hands on.

Lavallee isn't the only person to come away from Jean Lafitte's Blacksmith Shop with a supernatural experience. While sightings of the pirate himself are quite rare, all sorts of other phenomena have been reported at the bar over the years. Accounts of cold spots abound; more than one patron at the bar has turned at a tap on the shoulder only to find nobody there. Eyewitnesses claim to have caught the reflection of a pretty woman in a mirror upstairs. Lights have been known to flicker off on their own, and there are a number of accounts of extinguished candles alighting spontaneously in front of startled customers. It seems, then, that the pirate Jean Lafitte may not be the only ghost haunting the old building. Though, according to Lavallee, he must certainly be the most handsome.

The End